GUTE
LITERATURNOTEN!

GUTE LITERATURNOTEN!

GERMAN LITERATURE
ESSAY-WRITING

ROD HARES

HODDER AND STOUGHTON

LONDON SYDNEY AUCKLAND TORONTO

Also by Rod Hares:

Teaching French
Der deutsche Aufsatz (with C. G. Clemmetsen)
Compo! (with Genevieve Elliott)
Compo-Lit! French Literature essay-writing
Briefkasten
Comprehension for Advanced Level French

British Library Cataloguing in Publication Data
Hares, R. J.
    Gute Literaturnoten!: German literature—
essay-writing.
    1. German literature—History and criticism
    2. Criticism
    I. Title
    830.9   PT71

ISBN 0 340 37159 5

First published 1985
Second Impression 1987

Printed in Great Britain
for Hodder and Stoughton Educational
a division of Hodder and Stoughton Ltd, Mill Road
Dunton Green, Sevenoaks, Kent by
Page Bros (Norwich) Ltd

Phototypeset by Macmillan India Ltd., Bangalore–25.

I should like to dedicate this book to Nelson and Winnie Mandela and to the many others like them, who are never far from my thoughts, in the belief that good literature is one of the guardians of human freedom.

RJH

Acknowledgments

The author and publishers would like to thank the following for their kind permission to reproduce extracts from copyright material: Thomas Nelson & Sons Ltd for extracts from *Sansibar oder der letzte Grund* by Alfred Andersch; Lamuv-Verlag, Bornheim-Merten for an extract from *Wo warst du, Adam* by Heinrich Böll; Thomas Nelson & Sons Ltd for an extract from Episode am Genfer See by Stefan Zweig, from *Vier Novellen*; Methuen & Co. for an extract from *Der Hauptmann von Köpenick* by Carl Zuckmayer; from *Der kaukasische Kreidekreis* by Bertold Brecht copyright 1955 Suhrkamp Verlag, Frankfurt am Main, all rights reserved; Kessler-Verlag, Mannheim for extracts from *Die Bürger von Calais* by Georg Kaiser; Thomas Mann—*Der Tod in Venedig*—an excerpt by permission of S. Fischer Verlag GmbH, Frankfurt am Main; from *Mutter Courage und ihre Kinder* by Bertold Brecht copyright 1949 Suhrkamp Verlag, Frankfurt am Main, all rights reserved.

Every effort has been made to trace copyright holders; any rights not acknowledged here will be acknowledged in subsequent printings if notice is given to the publisher.

My considerable thanks are due to the following:
My wife, Lyn, for the proof-reading and for her patience.
Sue Scullard, Oxford College of Further Education, for her help with the poetry sections.
Peter Walker, ex-Northumberland College of Higher Education, for his general and illuminating thoughts on literature.
Derek Bowman, Edinburgh University, Albert Ward and Peter Thornton, Newcastle University, for their encouragement of Northumberland College students in their literature work.
Barbara Sietz, Goethe Institut, London, for her encouragement.
Rita Clarke, ex-Northumberland College, for her advice and support.
My daughters, Kate, Jackie, Julia and Antonia for the innumerable cups of coffee and their good humour.

Rod Hares

Contents

Foreword

German Literature Essay-Writing is a practical book, meant to help you over practical difficulties. Nonetheless, it would be dishonest not to admit another reason for writing this manual. I hope that the help you should find within these pages will enable you not only to write more effective literature essays, but also to gain greater enjoyment of your reading. A good book, like a good friend, is a companion to stay with us in times of trouble and to regale our spirits in times of happiness. May I wish you success in your writing and much joy in your reading!

Rod Hares

1

What is a German 'literature essay'?

What is a German 'literature essay'? This is a good question to ask yourself. A thoughtful answer will help you to achieve a sound approach to advanced essay-writing as part of the study of German literature. To find out exactly what the literature essay is, let us look at some of the more common traps into which students may fall, and which can be quite easily avoided. As a start, compare these short pieces written by two different individuals on the same essay topic:

> Essay title: *Discuss the prevailing atmosphere in Kafka's 'Der Prozeß' and 'Das Schloß'*

(a) In these books, K and Joseph K live in a bit of a dream-world. K gets arrested more or less at the bank, goes to a sort of tribunal for questioning, meets various people like the student, the whipper, the advocate, the manufacturer, the painter and so on and gets executed after a visit to a cathedral.

    Joseph K gets invited to the castle in the first place, arrives and spends the rest of his time trying to get out. They both give you the idea that they are always chasing all over the place and never getting anywhere, well, apart from the odd bit of help. You get the feeling the world they live in is a bit cruel and they're like guinea-pigs, though you couldn't put your finger on why.

(b) In 'Der Prozeß' and 'Das Schloß', Franz Kafka creates an environment for his main characters, which is highly reminiscent of the world of our dreams and even of our nightmares. Both K and Joseph K sense a mixture of reality and unreality in the bizarre succession of events which befall them, events which they are at a loss to control. Such occurrences are totally consistent with the oppressive, claustrophobic atmosphere, which threatens not only the two K's but others caught up with them.

    The atmosphere is compounded by the feeling of perpetual motion, of a frenzied chase, which we sense K and Joseph K are not meant to complete, despite the occasional outside intervention at the right moment. Another crucial component of the atmosphere is the sense of an impassive cruelty administered from above, to which the anti-heroes and their helpers are subjected without their or our ever knowing why.

Before you are given any more hints, you will already have seen some of the lessons for yourself. Example (a) is somewhat aimless and spends a dis-proportionate amount of time telling the story of the works, with not much attempt at analysis. Example (b) shows that the writer has set out to look further below the surface of the tales.

The key words are *story-telling* and *analysis*. The former is the most common fault found in literature essays and the latter is precisely what is required. If, before you start writing on a theme, you can discipline yourself not to fall into the trap of giving a 'potted account' of the events in the story, when what you are required to do is to *interpret* those events, you will have made a good beginning to your literary career.

Apart from the smoother style of example (b), which we shall leave for the moment, what is there about it which is *analytical* and makes it more worth reading than (a)? We can find this out by making a list of the specific points which show that the writer has sifted below the immediate surface of the novel. These are:

1. *Creates an environment . . . our nightmares.* The essayist states clearly what she feels to be the kernel of the theme. Note how the use of 'our' shows that the writer has realised the universality of Kafka's work. She is writing about us as well as about herself and the two K's.
2. *mixture of reality . . . which befall them* makes it clear that the situation is not wholly unreal and that there are real chords struck for the reader.
3. *at a loss to control . . . caught up with them.* The writer clearly understands that the bizarre events themselves are also part of the atmosphere. Additionally, she is careful to inform us that it is not just the K's who are threatened.
4. *perpetual motion . . . frenzied chase.* Unlike (a)'s reference to 'chasing all over the place', this phrase conveys more than a cliché. It tells us that the chase is both continuous and violently active.
5. *despite the occasional outside intervention.* The word 'outside' helps convey a feeling of strangeness and alienation.
6. *impassive cruelty.* 'Impassive' is an important qualifier and shows that the writer has understood the precise nature of whoever is controlling the situation.

This model, unlike the first example, attempts to interpret the work for the person reading the essay. Interpretation is, of course, closely related to analysis and to achieve this style of writing, you will find it helpful to write for your reader, as if he or she did not know the book and you were guiding them through the author's intentions without retelling the story.

If, you may well ask, you are expected to avoid telling the story of the book you are reading but are expected to be able to provide analysis, how precisely are you meant to achieve this?

Start by trying to view the work objectively, that is, by trying not to be too emotional in your reaction, and by attempting to look beneath the story line, so that you can see what is going on below. This is not easy. In fact, it can be very difficult, since books we read often produce a strong emotional response in us. However, a powerful reaction to a work can be put to good use. Ask yourself *why* you like the book so much, or feel angry at a specific character's behaviour or are greatly saddened by a particular event. Even at this early stage, a basic lesson is emerging.

If you can ask yourself not *what* happens, but *why* it happens, then you will have made an important early step towards a successful understanding of the work.

In order to help yourself to do this, you should understand that there are several basic processes operating in the complex relationship between a work and its reader. Among these processes, there are two vital ones which have not changed since they were identified by Classical Greek men of letters in the early days of literature. They are called *catharsis* and *vicarious action*.

CATHARSIS

Strictly speaking, the word *catharsis* means a purging of the emotions and derives from early Greek theatre, where drama was seen to serve the highly useful civic function of allowing audiences to give vent to potentially anti-social feelings such as anger, frustration, greed, violence. It was felt the citizens would return home contented after a visit to the theatre, their excess emotions drained, and in consequence, were more likely to remain calm and rational in their daily life.

Whatever the social benefits of drama, be it in Periclean Athens or down-town New York, the phenomenon known as catharsis will always function in a play or a work for reading, such as a novel or short story, provided the material is sufficiently gripping to involve the audience or readership to the extent that they feel taken out of themselves and identify with the characters and the events taking place.

An often-quoted example of the way in which a skilful craftsman can manipulate his audience into a strong personal involvement is reputed to have occurred during a performance of Shakespeare's *Othello* at Stratford. Once, when the play had reached the point where Othello was smothering Desdemona for apparently having been unfaithful to him with Iago, a member of the audience is said to have got up from his seat and shouted, 'Stop it, you fool! Can't you see she's innocent?'

This is a classic example of how a high emotional charge is generated in a person observing a fictional drama as it unfolds. The man concerned had become so involved that his emotions had crossed the line between fiction and reality. Catharsis is the drawing off of this emotional charge. It is something that we will often have experienced as we leave the cinema or switch off the television and find ourselves drained by the events we have watched.

The following passage from Alfred Andersch's *Sansibar oder der letzte Grund* is a good example of how the high emotional charge of the fictional situation and of the writing may transfer itself to the reader, who is given the position of the voyeur, witnessing an unpleasant situation with violent undertones:

(Judith, a Jewish girl, is in Rerik, trying to flee Germany in the last months before the Second World War. The landlord, recognising she is Jewish and requiring her identity card for formal purposes, intends to exploit her desperate position to his sexual advantage. He grabs the arm of a young Swedish sailor, who has invited Judith on board his ship.)

Der Schlager rauschte noch einmal auf und erlosch. Irgend jemand drehte das Radio ab. Der blonde Schwede hob seinen freien Arm und legte ihn auf das Handgelenk des Armes, mit dem der Wirt ihn gepackt hielt. Hoffentlich schlagen sie sich nicht, dachte Judith. Wenn es eine Schlägerei gibt, dann kommt die Polizei und dann werden alle Personalien festgestellt.

Aber der Wirt ließ von selbst seinen Arm sinken. Sie sind ja ein nettes Flittchen, sagte er zu Judith auf Deutsch. Sie wurde blaß. Der Schwede verstand nicht, was der Wirt zu Judith sagte, aber er erriet, daß er sie beschimpfte. Hör mal, sagte er, das Mädchen kann tun, was es will, und wenn du nicht deine Schnauze hältst . . .

Judith, die hinter dem Tisch hervorgetreten war, faßte ihn am Arm. Lassen Sie ihn, sagte sie. Aber es war deutlich, daß der Schwede und seine Kameraden jetzt eine Schlägerei wünschten. In diesem Augenblick rettete der graue junge Mann die Situation, indem er nach dem Wirt rief. Er rief mitten in die Stille hinein mit so scharfer, klarer Stimme, daß die Spannung zerfiel. Der Wirt trat aus dem Halbkreis und ging auf ihn zu.

Now you have read this extract, try to answer the following questions, giving reasons for your answers:

1 Do you feel negatively towards the landlord. If so, what emotions has he aroused and why?
2 What are your feelings for Judith?
3 How do you react at the end of the extract, when the landlord leaves Judith and the Swede and goes over to the grey young man's table?
4 How would you describe Judith's feelings during this scene?
5 What do you feel is Andersch's attitude to the scene depicted? Is it directly stated, or do we gather it by implication?

VICARIOUS ACTION OR INVOLVEMENT

The term *vicarious* is defined in the dictionary as *acting or doing for another*.

We have already seen how, when we read a good fictional work or follow a play of similar quality, a complex process develops. We become so immersed in events, at least for short periods of time, that we feel with or against the characters to the extent that the story might actually be taking place. We have accepted that our emotional response creates a form of catharsis, whereby our highly charged feelings are purged and we may even feel some conscious relief as a result of this process.

Vicarious involvement may be termed a form of *self-substitution* and occurs when our cathartic response to a work is strong enough for us to want to step inside the printed page and to become one of the characters. This is a most complex process, since we will often be totally unaware that it is happening.

Yet, most of us are cathartically involved almost every day of our lives, so much do we live off other people's experience as well as our own. All of us have our favourite works of fiction, plays, films, theatre, radio and television stories in which, at times, we will have identified so closely with one of the characters or with what (s)he is doing, that we might almost as well have been committing his or her actions ourselves. We will have *substituted* ourselves for that character.

For a few moments, we may have been the heroic figure in a tale of action, the beautiful woman casting a spell over those with whom she comes into contact, the millionaire spending his money so liberally, the recluse scientist working for humanity, the great philanthropist. Something inside us has wanted to pass over the barrier which separates us from the fictional character and we have substituted ourselves for that person.

However, the process is not always as obvious as in the case of the film buff crashing through the exit doors at the cinema, in the style of James Bond, or gliding demurely down the staircase, trailing shades of Scarlett O'Hara, the provocative heroine of *Gone With The Wind*.

There is a more common half-way position in which we may not actually become the characters who people the fictional world, but in which we identify very closely with some of their actions. In other words there is a degree of selectivity about our self-substitution.

Perhaps the best way to think of this is to be aware of the fact that readers are normally in the position of observers at the window. They are privileged to watch all that is going on, without ever being seen by the participants. From time to time the observers will be so touched by the events that, without entering into the personality of the characters, they will still feel as if they themselves are perpetrating some of the fictionalized actions. Let us look at another extract from *Sansibar*.

(The secret police have come to arrest Pfarrer Helander because of his lack of co-operation and of his involvement with the Resistance. Helander is a very sick man who is likely to die from gangrene, a complication of the amputation of one of his legs. He makes the decision to die fighting the secret police.)

Wie dumm von mir, dachte der Pfarrer, zu denken, ich schösse, um Gott zu züchtigen, Gott läßt mich schießen, weil er das Leben liebt.

Der erste, der hereinkam, war einer von den Zivilisten. Helander schoß ihn sofort nieder. Er kippte wie eine große Puppe nach hinten um, während sein Hut herunterfiel und langsam ins Zimmer rollte. In seinem schwarzen Ulster lag er über die Schwelle. Der zweite, der ihm hatte folgen wollen, einer der Uniformierten, hatte sich mit einem Sprung zurückgezogen.

Here we have a charged situation in which a man of God has made the conscious decision to kill. We sympathise with him and even approve his action, to the extent that when the uniformed policeman escapes, we hope that Helander will kill him too. This happens because Andersch has drawn such an effective picture of the evils of the Nazi state, that we are in sympathy with *all* resistance to it. Now, we even empathise with Helander, who is not the easiest of people with whom to get on.

Note what has happened. By skilful writing, the author has manipulated the reader into vicarious participation in deeds which in real life (s)he would not contemplate.

Thus, the writer's craft is partly one of manipulation, whereby the reader becomes an accomplice in a series of fictionalized actions. The better the writer, the better the manipulation. In any work that you study, ask yourself these fundamental questions:

1 How far does the author succeed in creating life-like characters and a believable world?
2 To what extent does the writer make me suspend my disbelief and allow the environment of the book to become a temporary real world in which I substitute myself from time to time?

DETACHMENT

Although we have considered catharsis and our own vicarious involvement in what we read, we should not look for an emotional charge and high reader involvement in every chapter or scene of a work of art. Heinrich Böll, appalled by the absurdity of war, appeals in *Wo warst du, Adam?* to our faculty of reason. Occasionally, in potentially harrowing circumstances, he will use humour to underline the ridiculousness of our behaviour and to allow us to stand outside the action. In the extract below, there is little chance of feeling we are in Greck's place.

(The German army is retreating, and Oberleutnant Dr Greck is in no position to follow his colleagues at the pace they require. He has eaten a large quantity of unripe apricots. With destruction by enemy bullets and mortar fire fairly imminent, Greck is trying to evacuate his bowels as he retreats)

Es waren noch dreihundert Meter bis zur Abfahrtsstelle, und durch das Geknalle hörte er manchmal, wie Major Krenz seinen Namen rief – aber es war ihm jetzt schon fast alles gleichgültig: er hatte Leibschmerzen, sehr, sehr heftige Leibschmerzen. Er hielt sich an der Mauer fest, während sein nacktes Gesaβ fror und in seinem Darm sich dieser wühlende Schmerz immer neu bildete wie langsam sich ansammelnder Explosionsstoff, der ungeheuerlich wirken würde, aber dann nur winzig blieb, sich immer wieder ansammelte, immer wieder die endgültige Befreiung zu bringen versprach . . .

This is a type of black humour, where we laugh at something, not because it is intrinsically funny, but through the *incongruity* of the situation. A somewhat inadequate and relatively harmless officer near to being killed by enemy fire, is more a target for sympathy than for laughter. But, Böll uses the 'caught with his trousers down' situation in a new way. We laugh when we should not, partly because of our own subconscious unease about private aspects of the self-grooming process. We recognise the unease in our laughter and then apply our reason to the whole situation. We may then reach a simple, but crucial conclusion. If men did not go in for ritual self-slaughter on a massive scale, Greck's silly little mistake in his quite pathetic life, when he has eaten unripe apricots, because his mother had trained him to keep his bowels regular, would not have final, destructive consequences. Why should someone have to die because he has eaten unripe fruit?

CHARACTER

One of your tasks will often be to assess the author's purpose as seen through his attitude to his characters. This can take a number of forms. For example, in Stefan Zweig's Novelle, *Buchmendel*, his attitude to Jakob Mendel comes through clearly:

> Jetzt erst, älter geworden, verstand ich, wieviel mit jedem solchen Menschen verschwindet, erstlich weil alles Einmalige von Tag zu Tag kostbarer wird in unserer rettungslos einförmiger werdenden Welt.

Through the narrator, Zweig shows his admiration and affection for worthwhile, resolute eccentrics like Mendel, the old bookseller, who embodies the values of a fast-disappearing world.

An author's compassion for his characters may be less directly stated. One device used, is to make us feel for a character through the reaction (s)he provokes in someone else. In *Der Richter und sein Henker*, for example, the thoughts and actions of the doctor and old school-friend, who has to admit to Bärlach that he has a year to live at most, arouse considerable sympathy in us for the latter:

> 'Nur noch ein Jahr,' antwortete Hungertobel, setzte sich an der Wand seines Ordinationszimmers auf einen Stuhl und sah hilflos zu Bärlach hinüber, der in der Mitte des Zimmers stand, in ferner, kalter Einsamkeit, unbeweglich und demütig, vor dessen verlorenem Blick der Arzt nun die Augen senkte.

You should be aware that the author's attitude to his characters is important, not simply because it shows how he feels about his creations, but also because it will often reveal his purpose in writing the work. A main character may be like Wenzel Strapinski in Keller's *Kleider machen Leute*, a basically honest innocent abroad, undergoing a wide variety of experiences, some of them unpleasant, who eventually matures to a reasonable degree of self-knowledge and to a point where he may reflect the sounder values of society, or, alternatively, show how society needs to be changed.

Bertolt Brecht's *Mutter Courage* is, as her name implies, a woman of immense courage, who plies her trader's waggon through a significant portion of the Hundred Years' War, making a living for herself, her children, and the others who rely on her. Her reactions are sometimes crude, sometimes instinctive, not infrequently highly rational and perceptive. By the way she continues to endure, despite the loss of her children, a potential new husband and virtually all of her prosperity, she symbolises Brecht's belief in the common folk and, as important, his conviction that the ordinary people are the cannon-fodder for a relentless military machine:

> Manchmal seh ich mich schon durch die Höll fahrn mit mein Planwagen und Pech verkaufen oder durchn Himmel, Wegzehrung ausbieten an irrende Seelen. Wenn ich mit meine Kinder, wo mir verblieben sind, eine Stell fänd, wo nicht herumgeschossen würd, möcht ich noch ein paar ruhige Jahr haben.

A character may reflect very closely the author's own predicament, or, at least the predicament of a group with whom he or she identifies very closely. In Thomas Mann's work, for instance, a main theme is the role of the artist in society. To what extent is the highly creative individual a fully-fledged member of society and in what measure is (s)he an outside observer, alienated by his or her own ability to perceive? This is a question of great significance for Mann, himself a highly creative artistic talent. Consequently, in *Der Tod in Venedig* and *Tonio Kröger*, we cannot but be aware of his feeling for the artistic main characters. When Tonio thinks back on the two people of his adolescence who meant so much to him, the enthusiasm and emotionalism in his thoughts make us feel that Thomas Mann knows his characters only too well, since they are people and they voice thoughts which reflect his own predicament in at least some measure:

> Hatte ich euch vergessen? fragte er. Nein, niemals! Nicht dich, Hans, noch dich, blonde Inge! Ihr wart es ja, für die ich arbeitete, und wenn ich Applaus vernahm, blickte ich heimlich um mich, ob ihr daran teilhättet . . .

This example has been deliberately chosen to illustrate a point which we would do well to remember. When passages occur which clearly have some auto-biographical relevance, it is too easy to assume that they are an *exact* reflection of the author and of his or her own experience. Try to remember that, great affection as an author like Thomas Mann may have for his Tonio Kröger, the character and the novelle, itself, are fictional creations and will rarely be an exact reflection of the author's own life and experiences.

ASSIGNMENTS

1 Choose a character from a German work and try to show what the author thinks of him/her.
2 Select a character from a book you have read and show how (s)he fits in with the author's purpose.
3 Often, an author's attitude to his characters will not be especially clear, since he will wish not to intrude, so do not expect to be able to deduce his reactions. Instead, concentrate on asking yourself how *you* feel about the characters. Think of a character in one of your set books and try to find 4–6 examples in the text to show why you feel one of the following emotions towards him/her:

affection/dislike/sympathy/scorn/pride/resentment/envy/disbelief/anger/amusement/derision/disgust.

Character analysis is dealt with in full in Chapter 6, but, for the moment, it may be helpful to refer to the character-profile checklist on page 48.

ATMOSPHERE

Another key factor which needs to be taken into account is the prevailing atmosphere within the book. This will give you a good indication of some of the author's reasons for writing. In *Der Prozeß*, the atmosphere is tense and hermetic. There is a feeling of claustrophobia, never more apparent than in the courtroom, where **K**.'s investigation begins:

> K. glaubte in eine Versammlung einzutreten. Ein Gedränge der verschiedensten Leute – niemand kümmerte sich um den Eintretenden – füllte ein mittelgroßes, zweifenstriges Zimmer, das knapp an der Decke von einer Galerie umgeben war, die gleichfalls vollständig besetzt war und wo die Leute nur gebückt stehen konnten und mit Kopf und Rücken an die Decke stießen.

The resulting ambiance helps convey the psychological and spiritual crisis which K, in many ways symbolical of modern man and woman, is undergoing.

Whenever you have to assess the prevailing atmosphere within the work you are studying, use the checklist below to help you:

ATMOSPHERE

Place a tick in the box opposite each adjective you feel describes the atmosphere of the book in question:

Quality	√	Page Ref.		√	Page Ref.
affectionate			insecure		
anxious			lacking feeling		
calm			morbid		
claustrophobic			optimistic		
coarse			passionate		
dead			pessimistic		
despairing			petty		
dramatic			relaxed		
empty			relieved		
energetic			resentful		
exuberant			reverential		
farcical			sad		
forbidding			scandalous		
gay			secure		
glamorous			serious		
guilt-ridden			sinister		
happy			slow		
hopeful			soporific		
humble			soulless		
humorous			sophisticated		
inert			tense		
innocent			tragic		
			violent		
Additions:			warm		

ASSIGNMENT

Study each short passage and choose from the alternatives what sort of atmosphere you think is being built up. Give reasons for your decision.

(a) *Die Verwandlung* Franz Kafka
(Gregor Samsa wakes up to find he has turned into a beetle. He is trying to unlock the bedroom door to let in his mother and the company secretary.)

Dann aber machte er sich daran, mit dem Mund den Schlüssel im Schloß umzudrehen. Es schien leider, daß er keine eigentlichen Zähne hatte, – womit sollte er gleich den Schlüssel fassen? – aber dafür waren die Kiefer freilich sehr stark; mit ihrer Hilfe brachte er auch wirklich den Schlüssel in Bewegung und achtete nicht darauf, daß er sich zweifellos irgendeinen Schaden zufügte, denn eine braune Flüssigkeit kam ihm aus dem Mund, floß über den Schlüssel und tropfte auf den Boden.

guilt-ridden/humble/pathetic/soulless

(b) *Maria Stuart* Friedrich Schiller
(The rival cousins Mary, Queen of Scots, and Elisabeth I meet while the fate of the prisoner Mary hangs in the balance. They are both women of great strength and passion.)

ELISABETH: Es kostet nichts, die allgemeine Schönheit
    Zu sein, als die gemeine sein für alle!
MARIA: Das ist zu viel!
ELISABETH (*höhnisch lachend*): Jetzt zeigt Ihr Euer wahres
    Gesicht, bis jetzt wars nur die Larve.

highly charged/anxious/sad/inert

(c) *Aus dem Leben eines Taugenichts* Joseph von Eichendorff
(Taugenichts, having been told to leave home by his father, who is tired of his idleness, sets off into the wide world.)

Hinter mir gingen nun Dorf, Gärten und Kirchtürme unter, vor mir neue Dörfer, Schlösser und Berge auf; unter mir Saaten, Büsche und Wiesen bunt vorüberfliegend, über mir unzählige Lerchen in der klaren blauen Luft – ich schämte mich laut zu schreien, aber innerlich jauchzte ich und strampelte und tanzte auf dem Wagentritt herum.

soporific/joyful/calm/impersonal

(d) *Bahnwärter Thiel* Gerhart Hauptmann
(Thiel is a railway-crossing keeper, who lives very much in his own mind. One wet and misty night, the lights of a train moving through the damp, black night provoke a vision.)

Zwei rote, runde Lichter durchdrangen wie die
Glotzaugen eines riesigen Ungetüms die Dunkelheit.
Ein blutiger Schein ging vor ihnen her, der die Regentropfen in seinem Bereich in Blutstropfen verwandelte. Es war, als fiele ein Blutregen vom Himmel.

coarse/resentful/sinister/reverential

(e) *Dame am Steuer* Gertrud Fussenegger
(The woman at the wheel drives recklessly through the night as a form of escape from her man, Fedja, with whom there is no real contact.)

Da muß ich fahren, Fedja. An Ausreden fehlt es mir nicht, wenn du sie mir auch nicht mehr glaubst, diese armseligen Lügen. Auch heute belog ich dich: ich wollte Ruth besuchen, meine Schwester, die krank ist. Ja, krank ist sie; trotzdem besuch ich sie nicht, und du weißt es, weißt, daß ich Ruth nicht mag, daß ich im Grunde niemand mag, nicht einmal – dich.

energetic/confused/far-fetched/despairing

(f) *Bekanntschaft mit einem Handwerk* – Stefan Zweig
(The narrator has observed a man acting strangely on the street. Eventually, contact will be made between the two men, but, for the moment, the narrator observes and wonders.)

Donnerwetter, was suchst du eigentlich, Kerl? Auf was, auf wen wartest du da? Ein Bettler, das bist du nicht . . . Ein Arbeiter bist du auch nicht, denn die haben Schlag elf Uhr vormittags keine Gelegenheit hier so lässig herumzulungern . . . Also Schluß, was suchst du da?

forbidding/neutral/full of suspense/pessimistic

THE BACKCLOTH

A related element is the background against which the main events are set. The characters may play out their lives in a city or a small town, in the countryside or at sea, in isolation or in contact with people. They will live in an environment which may be hostile/frenzied/inhospitable/sedate/welcoming/strange/very familiar or many other things.

Whatever its particular quality, it is likely to have a discernible effect on one or more of the main characters in the book. Always try to establish what exactly the effect is of the environment in which individuals find themselves placed.

If the influence of the environment is sufficiently strong to determine the way in which a character behaves, as, for instance in much of the work of Anna Seghers or the early output of Heinrich Böll, then the author's approach is said to be *deterministic*, i.e. the character's behaviour is determined by his or her surroundings. In Böll's *Die blasse Anna*, for example, there is something aimless about the soldier who returns to his home town after the Second World War and several years as a prisoner:

Erst im Frühjahr 1950 kehrte ich aus dem Krieg heim und ich fand niemanden mehr in der Stadt, den ich kannte. Zum Glück hatten meine Eltern mir Geld hinterlassen. Ich mietete ein Zimmer in der Stadt, dort lag ich auf dem Bett, rauchte und wartete. Arbeiten zu gehen, hatte ich keine Lust. Ich gab meiner Wirtin Geld, und sie kaufte alles für mich und bereitete mir das Essen.

It is hardly surprising that, after the harrowing experiences of war and internment, a youngish man returning to a town in which he is now a stranger, should become an isolate. This was the fate of very many people in the immediate post-war Germany.

In *Sansibar*, Judith's anxiety, her lack of confidence and her almost total insecurity have obvious roots. Andersch uses her and her background to symbolise aspects of the whole Jewish problem, of what a race threatened with extinction had to endure. Judith's mother commits suicide, in order to give her daughter the chance to escape:

> Als sie [Judith] in den Salon zurückkam, war Mama tot. Sie war über dem Tisch zusammengesunken, und in der rechten Hand hielt sie noch die Tasse, aus der sie das Gift getrunken hatte. Judith hatte die Reste der geleerten Kapsel in der Tasse gesehen und gewußt, daß nichts mehr zu machen war.

Note that in both these extracts, the environment and the prevailing atmosphere tell us a great deal about the way in which people in general were living. Any well-written work of fiction will give us such insights through the background employed to explain the circumstances of specific individual characters.

ASSIGNMENTS

Study each of the following short extracts and try to assess the relationship between backcloth and character.

(a) *Episode am Genfer See – Stefan Zweig*
(In the summer of 1918, a fleeing Russian soldier is found in Lake Geneva by some of the local Swiss. Here is part of his story, told to an interpreter.)

> Er hatte in Rußland gekämpft, war dann eines Tages mit tausend andern in Waggons verpackt worden und sehr weit gefahren, dann wieder in Schiffe verladen und noch länger mit ihnen gefahren durch Gegenden, wo es so heiß war, wie er sich ausdrückte, einem die Knochen im Fleisch weichgebraten wurden. Schließlich waren sie irgendwo wieder gelandet und in Waggons verpackt worden und hatten dann mit einemmal einen Hügel zu stürmen, worüber er nichts Näheres wußte, weil ihn gleich zu Anfang eine Kugel ins Bein getroffen habe. Den Zuhörern, denen der Dolmetsch Rede und Antwort übersetzte, war sofort klar, daß dieser Flüchtling ein Angehöriger jener russischen Divisionen in Frankreich war, die man über die halbe Erde, über Sibirien und Wladiwostok an die französische Front geschickt hatte.

What is your reaction to the Russian refugee/deserter, once you have heard his background? What general point do you think Zweig is suggesting?

(b) *Der Traktorist – Anna Seghers*
(It is the early years of the East German communes after the Second World War. Young Geschke has lost his leg as the result of a tractor accident and is

impatient to return to his work. His friend, Hans, tells him about another badly-injured tractor-driver to encourage him.)

Ich habe gehört, in Weilsbach der beste Traktorist, der hat auch bloß ein Bein. Der hat seins im Krieg verloren. Man hat ihm eine besondere Prothese gemacht, sie sagen, so schön, wie sein Bein war. Extra dafür hat man ihm einen Traktor ummontiert, und er ist jetzt ihr bester Traktorist.

What does this extract suggest about the spirit and mentality of East German farm workers? What does it tell us about the social purposes of immediate post-war (and later) fiction in that country?

(c) *Der Hauptmann von Köpenick – Carl Zuckmayer*
(Voigt has spent much of his life in prison. His brother-in-law, Hoprecht, is attempting to persuade him to accept the ethics and the implications of Prussian Germany, at the turn of the century. Voigt cannot expect it to be easy to regain work and respect. He must bear his burden.)

HOPRECHT: Du mußt das tragen – wie 'n Mann.
VOIGT: Tragen – das bin ick gewohnt, Friedrich. Das macht mir nichts. Ich hab' 'nen breiten Buckel, da geht ein Packen 'rauf. Aber-*wohin* soll ick's tragen, Friedrich! Das ist die Frage! Wo soll ick denn hin damit? Ick hab' ja keinen Aufenthalt, für mir gibt's ja keinen Platz auf der Erde, da könnt' ick höchstens in die Luft mit steigen, nich?
HOPRECHT: Nich in die Luft, Willem! Zurück auf den Boden, Mensch! Wir leben in 'nem Staat, – und wir leben in 'ner Ordnung, – da kannst du dir nich außerhalb stellen, das darfst du nich! So schwer's auch hält, – da *mußt* du dich wieder 'rein fügen!
VOIGT: Wo 'rein? In den Staat? In 'ne Ordnung? Ohne Aufenthalt? Und ohne Paß?

What do you learn from this extract of the characters and attitudes of the two men? How do you react to Voigt's predicament and how do you see the position of ex-criminals in the Germany of 1900?

THE HISTORICAL BACKGROUND

Wherever possible, you should take the historical background of the work into account, as this may have a material effect on (a) its subject matter, (b) your interpretation of it.

To prove the point, look at this extract from Erich Kästner's *Die Konferenz der Tiere*, which expresses most strongly the author's revulsion against war and the militarism which causes it. In this tale, mankind has once again refused to reach consensus at a disarmament conference, so the animals decide that they must give a lead, by holding their own conference, at which positive, humanitarian decisions will be made:

> Oskar und Alois und Leopold und viel andere Delegierte hatten die Wagenfenster heruntergelassen und winkten mit ihren Taschentüchern. Und die Mütter mit den Elefäntchen und den anderen Tierkindern winkten zurück. 'Blamiert euch nicht!' rief Oskars Frau mit erhobenem Rüssel. 'Keine Bange!' schrie Oskar zurück. 'Wir werden die Welt schon in Ordnung bringen! Wir sind ja schließlich keine Menschen!'

This short extract gives something of the flavour of Kästner's tale. The story will always have universal implications, since it deals with the abiding theme of war, triggered by human aggression. Thus, a reader from our own time will recognize its implications for their very universality and will probably smile at the whimsical feel of the tale – anthropomorphism gently running riot. But, set against the time of its writing, we see that it contains topical references to the failure of a whole string of peace initiatives. It is a strong plea for us to withstand totalitarianism and it is defiantly anti-Hitler. This is a brave story written by a courageous man.

As far as method is concerned, Kästner has situated his story in a parallel world of animals and human beings, so we will perceive symbolical meaning in the action. The events that occur, despite the apparent fairy-tale atmosphere, symbolize current, or likely future events and the universality of human behaviour.

Do not take the 'historical' in the title of this section too literally, despite the example. 'Historical' may simply relate to the history of the author, rather than to that of the world. Alternatively, as in the case of Heinrich Böll, the writer may use his or her very common experience to write of events which many others will recognise in their own lives. In every tale of Böll's which features soldiers returning homewards at the end of the war, there will be shades of his own experiences as a returnee:

> Als er am anderen Morgen wieder aufs Dach stieg, gegen acht, schien er schon Monate, fast Jahre dort zu sein. Die Stille und die Einsamkeit waren selbstverständlich.

Here, a note of warning should be sounded. Beware the temptation to see characters and events as exact replicas of the author's own past. This is a rare occurrence in fact, since his craft is to *create* out of his own experience.

When you discover parallels between the author's life and the subject-matter of the work, make sure you connect them in your own writing, at least in passing, since awareness of them helps towards a greater understanding of the book.

ASSIGNMENT

Study any background notes available on the author of one of your set books. Then, look through the text and try to find at least three passages in which his or her own character and experiences are clearly reflected.

THE STYLE

It is important to be able to assess the implications of the author's style of writing, if you are to achieve a full understanding of the work. The next chapter deals with this in detail.

ASSIGNMENTS

1 Choose a main character from one of your set books and, using short quotations, show how his/her character develops or remains static during the course of the work.

2 Select 4–6 example passages in a book you are studying to illustrate any *one* of the following qualities in a character of your choice:

   sympathetic/distant/weak/overbearing/comic/tragic/violent/irrational/impulsive/proud/wise/humanitarian/kind/inadequate/anxious/carefree/evil.

3 Look back at the list of qualities in Assignment 2 and name for each one any character you have encountered who fits the description.

4 Think of an unpleasant character in a set book. Try to locate instances in the text, which show him/her to have redeeming characteristics.

5 Is there any character you have encountered in German literature whose behaviour sometimes seems markedly inconsistent with his/her normal actions? Find example passages in the text to prove your point.

6 Find a character to whom you relate very positively. Give short examples from the text to show why you like him/her.

7 Do the same for a character whom you dislike.

8 Choose a character from a set book, who reminds you of someone you have seen in a film. Make notes on their similarities.

9 Find a character in real life who resembles one of the characters in a German book you have read. Make notes on their similarities.

10 Are you able to find a character in a set book who is simply not true to life? Give 4–6 short examples of his/her behaviour to prove your point.

11 Study the behaviour of a character in a set book and describe where it is typically German.

12 Do you know a work in which any main character resembles the author? Find 3–4 sample passages to support your view.

13 If any main character resembles a famous historical person, find passages in the work which illustrate this similarity.

14 Find any main character who, you feel, fails to come off. Find examples in the text to show why.

15 Find 4–6 example passages in which one of your authors uses physical description to convey character.

16 Is there a conflict between the characters of two of the main protagonists in any of the German books that you have read? If so, find 3–5 points of contrast between the two people.

17 Is there a character in any of your set books who is essentially tragic? Draw examples from the text to show exactly what it is which makes the individual tragic.

2

The author's style

What is style, apart from something which is difficult to define? However different writers such as Thomas Mann, Andersch, Dürrenmatt, Zweig, Grass may be, they all have a style of their own. Indeed, it is this very difference which is the essence of the phenomenon we are attempting to define.

Style is an author's personal identifier, his or her set of fingerprints, something characteristic about the way the words have been put down on paper, something so individual and recognizable that a seasoned reader can often identify a writer from a few lines of print he has never seen before.

We ourselves often use the word *style* in a non-literary way, when we say that a person *has style*. What we mean is that the individual we are referring to has something special about him, which marks him out from the crowd, so that we notice him and, even more important, want to notice him, since he brings brightness and life to a scene which may be very run-of-the-mill.

This colloquial definition is not as far removed from the literary implications of the term as it may at first appear. When you are required to analyse an author's style, a good starting point is to ask yourself what it is that is special about the way Böll or Siegfried Lenz writes, what it is which makes them stand out from the crowd of pulp-writers.

By definition, any of the writers you are required to study will have reached the respectability of the A-level study lists, because there is something about them which is special. Apart from the fact that their work will be significant or socially committed or psychologically relevant, it will have an attractiveness, a readability, which draw the literati to it.

The style will be the general feel or texture of what the author writes, but it is difficult to generalize and, fortunately, not necessary here, since we can identify those elements of which an author's style is composed. They are:

THE GENERAL QUALITY OF THE WORK

When we read a book simply for pleasure, we do not sift the various elements of style into separate compartments. Rather, we read the story and are left with a general, overall impression of the way the author writes. This should be the starting point for any essay on style. The first question to ask yourself should be *What is my general impression of the way the author writes?* You are likely to decide on one of the following qualities or something similar. The work may be:

optimistic   – throughout, or perhaps despite certain unfortunate events, the author sees hope in the future.

pessimistic   – the overriding impression is one of gloom. Initiative seems pointless.

epic   – the tale is set in a time or against a background of great events.

small-scale   – the author is concerned with ordinary people from an equally ordinary background. There is no attempt to imply universal significance.

impersonal   – there is little attempt by the writer to intervene or to communicate his or her attitude.

involved   – here, the author intervenes either directly or by allusion.

committed   – events within the narrative arouse our sense of justice or of social conscience, as is the author's main purpose in writing.

celebratory   – there is a feeling of *joie de vivre*, of lightness, spontaneity, rich satisfaction, exultation.

disillusioned   – the work is written in muted tones, with little signs of great bitterness or its opposite. There may be much unpleasant conflict between characters.

ASSIGNMENT

Start an essay on style, by deciding which one or more of the above qualities best represent(s) the feel of any work you have read. Write down the attribute(s) and find 2–4 page references to back up your judgment.

NARRATIVE STYLE

Whichever quality you decide is the hallmark of the work, it will have been fostered by the use of one or more of the following narrative styles:

personal   – full of comments which obviously come from the author, or of references to his or her own experience.

detached   – there is no attempt by the author to let his or her feelings intrude.

detailed   – the narrative contains much description, often very painstaking and detailed in its accuracy.

impression-istic   – by contrast, the writer only sketches out the detail or background. A little has to go a long way.

evocative   – details are often vivid enough to conjure up memories in the reader, or to stimulate quite intense feeling.

direct   – the approach is rather matter-of-fact. Detail is given and thoughts are stated in a straightforward manner.

ironic   – the author highlights discrepancies in behaviour or in a situation. What actually occurs is often radically different from professed views or accepted standards of behaviour.

pathetic	– pathos is used to *tug at the reader's heartstrings.* As this cliché implies, it is all too easy for pathos to be overdone and to descend into bathos or sentimentality.
humorous	– significant amounts of humour and comedy may be employed, possibly either as a reflection of the author's attitude to life, or to lighten the implications of a serious message.
serious	– aware of the weight of implications in what (s)he is writing, the author finds little room for humorous distraction.
popular	– this narrative style is not to be confused with the use of humour. Through a wish to communicate directly with a broader readership, the writer may employ a style which sometimes borders on the colloquial. Such a style may also be a reaction to other writers regarded as over-pretentious.
erudite	– the opposite of a popular style, this quality indicates an author who cannot help scattering learned references throughout the text, or using a great deal of intellectual vocabulary and imagery.
loose	– an author is said to have a loose style, when (s)he appears to have written rather carelessly without taking the trouble to link ideas and themes.
tightly constructed	– here, nothing is left to chance, almost every detail seems to be of significance and has to earn its inclusion. The plot and themes are closely and neatly worked through to a precise conclusion.

ASSIGNMENT

As with the previous assignment, decide which qualities best describe the narrative style of a work you are currently studying. Write them down and, once again, find 2–4 page references to back up your judgement.

THE STYLE OF THE LANGUAGE

The style of the language used will inevitably reflect the particular general qualities from those above, which characterize the work. Among the types of expression you will have to identify are:

terse	– this is a clipped style, where no more details or words are used than necessary. Consequently, the narrative moves along very quickly.
prolix	– this is the opposite quality, regarded as a defect. The style is wordy and weighed down with unnecessary detail. The reader may feel impatient with the author.
dense	– this attribute should not be confused with prolixity. Certain authors (most notably, Thomas Mann) link ideas and expression closely, often to convey an impression of the complexity of the human relationships which they are attempting to portray.

light	– does not mean superficial. The author employs bright, lively imagery, with touches of humour. The overall effect is often good-humoured, entertaining and likely to make the reader smile with the author and his/her characters, without the need to think too deeply.
lyrical	– the language is carefully chosen in an attempt to create an emotional, usually uplifting response in the reader. In a prose work, such lines will strike you as rather poetic.
prosaic	– the opposite of lyrical, this may be a deliberate device on the part of the author to reflect through the mundane nature of the language and theme, the tediousness of the existences portrayed in the work.
lively	– the author may structure his/her ideas so that the narrative proceeds very rapidly. The style of language may change from character to character and from situation to situation, so that the reader is caught up in a rapid process.
dramatic	– the language is direct and at times even a little exaggerated, to mirror a fast-moving situation, where the reader is involved in great or at least important events.
unstressed	– the author deliberately suppresses emotive language and the narrative proceeds on a monotonous level, often through the use of a standard, almost unvarying sentence pattern.
romantic	– (See the definition of German Romanticism on page 71) This does not simply imply the rosy glow of a tale of love. There may, indeed, be much blood and thunder, or the suggestion of it, provided that the detail never becomes realistic enough to bring us back to the actual world we inhabit.
realistic	– the opposite of romantic. Images and speech are deliberately structured to present a view of life as it is lived. The style may even cause offence through its directness, e.g. by the use of obscene language.

ASSIGNMENTS

1 Decide which adjectives best describe the style of the language used by an author you are studying. Write them down and this time find at least half a dozen page references to back your judgement.

2 In a short chapter, it is impossible to list in detail all the stylistic devices an author might use. We have worked through the broad areas. Now, with the aid of a dictionary and more important, discussion with your fellow students and teachers, make notes on the following items we have not discussed:

The use of
allegory
allusion
anthropomorphism

antithesis
apostrophe
bathos
contrast
contemporary reference
dramatic irony
ellipsis
historical figures
implication
invective
jargon
listing
oxymoron
parable
sarcasm
symbol

In the course of the next year, try to find at least one example of every one of the above devices in your German reading!

3 For each of the short extracts, answer the multiple-choice question below it. In each case, there is only one appropriate answer.

(a) *Eine, die es mal nicht eilig hat, dachte der Wirt. Solche Mädchen hatten es meistens eilig, zu den Kirchen zu kommen. Die hier schien nicht so eifrig zu sein. Mal eine Ausnahme. Eine hübsche und ziemlich junge Ausnahme übrigens.*

Andersch: *Sansibar oder der letzte Grund*

The . . . . nature of the language reflects the landlord's basic, uncomplicated character.
1 lively
2 lyrical
3 direct and staccato
4 prolix.

(b) *Herrlich an jenem merkwürdigen Aprilmorgen 1931 war schon die nasse, aber bereits wieder durchsonnte Luft. Wie ein Seidenbonbon schmeckte sie süß, kühl, feucht und glänzend, gefilterter Frühling, unverfälschtes Ozon . . .*

Zweig: *Bekanntschaft mit einem Handwerk*

Zweig's description of the April morning strikes . . . . note which is maintained through the early stages of the tale.
1 an optimistic
2 a reflective
3 a serious
4 a dramatic.

(c) *Das ganze Jahr 1635 ziehen Mutter Courage und ihre Tochter Kattrin über die Landstraßen Mitteldeutschlands folgend den immer zerlumpteren Heeren.*

Brecht: *Mutter Courage und ihre Kinder*

The titles at the beginning of each scene underline the . . . . nature of the backcloth to Courage's tale.
1 romantic
2 humorous
3 evocative
4 epic.

(d) *Etwas Amtlich-Erzieherisches trat mit der Zeit in Gustav von Aschenbachs Vorführungen ein, sein Stil entriet in späteren Jahren der unmittelbaren Kühnheiten, der subtilen und neuen Abschattungen, er wandelte sich ins Mustergültig-Feststehende, . . .*

Mann: *Der Tod in Venedig*

The . . . . tone of the language parallels the change in Aschenbach's character.
1 official, formal
2 languid
3 detached
4 evocative.

(e) *Sie waren noch nie aus diesem Dorf herausgekommen, und wenn es einer mal tun mußte, dann traf er gleich Vorbereitungen, als ob er zu einem andern Stern reisen wollte. Vielleicht glaubten einige sogar, daß die Welt hinter den Feldern von Romeiken zu Ende sei. Das mag schon sein.*

Lenz: *Lotte soll nicht sterben*

This is a . . . . comment by the author on an isolated community.
1 part sympathetic, part ironic
2 sarcastic
3 romantic
4 allegorical.

(f) *Ich bin inzwischen vielen Menschen begegnet, im Theater und im Kino, im Klub und beim Stammtisch, die bestimmt nicht sie selber waren, sondern bereits ihre mechanischen Doppelgänger.*

Kasack: *Mechanischer Doppelgänger*

Could key personnel already have been replaced by mechanical doubles? Are such creatures science-fiction or secret, scientific fact? Kasack ends the tale on a typically . . . . note.
1 credible.
2 contentious.
3 serious
4 whimsical.

(g) *Er war ganz erfüllt von Jugend und Daseinfreude, und diese Freude galt nicht nur dem eigenen Dasein, nicht nur dem Stück Erde, das er pflügte, sondern der Erde schlechthin. Sie reichte im Morgendunst, so weit sein Blick reichte.*

Seghers: *Der Traktorist*

In this extract Anna Seghers is at pains to underline the . . . . of the youthful tractor driver.

1 resignation
2 disillusionment
3 optimism
4 pessimism.

(h) *Dieser Karan hatte ein finsteres Aussehen. Sein Bart hing in zwei schwarzen öligen Sicheln zu beiden Seiten des wülstigen Mundes bis zum Hals herab. Seine Haupthaare, die trotz des Alters dunkel geblieben waren, hingen lang wie die Haare einer Frau, in der Mitte gescheitelt, von Schmutz starrend.*

Rinser: *Die gläsernen Ringe*

Luise Rinser uses physical description to . . . .
1 invoke a sympathetic response
2 imply character
3 provide variety
4 create a lively atmosphere.

(i) *'Merkwürdig,' sagte Bärlach, dabei arbeiten die doch wie wild.'. . . . . sagte Lutz: 'ich weiß, daß Sie immer bereit sind, Kommissär Bärlach, einen Fehlgriff gegen die großen Erkenntnisse der modernen wissenschaftlichen Kriminalistik zu beschönigen.'*

Dürrenmatt: *Der Richter und sein Henker*

Dürrenmatt uses the two men's conversational styles to underline their . . . . characters.
1 similar
2 contrasting
3 complementary
4 sophisticated.

(j) *Die Gäste rührten sich nicht. Ellen wandte sich hilfesuchend nach ihnen um. In diesem Augenblick sahen alle den Stern an ihrem Mantel. Einzelne lachten hönisch. Die andern hatten ein mitleidiges Lächeln um den Mund. Keiner half ihr.*

Aichinger: *Die größere Hoffnung*

Ilse Aichinger uses a pattern of short, sharp sentences to underline the young Jewess's predicament and to . . . .
1 build the tension
2 develop character
3 reassure the reader.
4 convey the friendly atmosphere.

3

Structuring the essay

The way you structure your essay is crucial both to the impression it will make upon your reader and to its final success. You should not think of an essay's success simply in terms of the level of mark it obtains. An essay is a creation which has stemmed from your own brain. Therefore a good composition is an achievement in its own right, of which you should be justifiably proud.

In order for such a work to be worthy of merit, it has to be well planned and set out, so that those who judge it will be impressed by its clarity and balance. In other words, if there is a clear and logical structure to the essay, your readers will have no trouble in understanding what you are putting forward as a thesis. The material below should help you achieve that sought-after precision.

PLANNING REQUIREMENTS AND RESTRICTIONS

LENGTH

It is difficult to provide anything more than a guideline as to length, but the manageable limits for a non-examination essay would be 3–8 sides of A4, depending on the complexity and scope of the subject. Of this 20–25 per cent might be quotation. In the exam situation 10–20 per cent quotation is a realistic expectation.

ANSWERING THE QUESTION

The onus is on you to deal specifically with the issue(s) raised in the title. Irrelevant material will not gain credit. Neither will an answer where you decide that the title is not to your taste and substitute a theme of your own choosing. For example, if you have been asked to contrast the two queens in *Maria Stuart*, an analysis of Maria's character alone will not do.

Another typical deviation from the norm is to take a slightly obscure quotation in a title to mean what you want it to mean, so that it will fit nicely with the material you have prepared (see pages 41–2).

STICKING TO YOUR THEME

This point is dealt with on page 97 of Chapter 12.

TEXTUAL REFERENCE

When you make general points, try to give specific examples. This will not only show that you know a work reasonably well, but will help the reader see the point you are making (see page 98).

UNDERSTANDING

Your brief is to show that you have understood the implications of the work. It will help you in the structuring of your essay, if, instead of thinking simply about the story-line, you keep reminding yourself of the author's purpose in writing and how (s)he achieves it.

READER INTEREST

It is crucial that you keep in mind the need to interest the person looking at your essay. Even if you feel you do not have any ideas which are startlingly new (and very few people will), you can give your writing a reasonably fresh appearance by varying your vocabulary and the length of your sentences and paragraphs.

Try also to think of some topical event, or of a film or another book, etc, with which you may draw parallels. This all helps to make your reader feel that occasionally something different is being said.

MAKING A PLAN

When you are producing the first rough outline of your essay try to find
  (a) 6–8 major points;
  (b) 1–3 textual illustrations of each of these points;
  (c) a suitable order for the points, ending on a strong note;
  (d) other works by your author or by another, with which parallels may be drawn;
  (e) quotations from the text to support your argument.

TYPES OF STRUCTURE

The way an essay is put together is crucial to its success. Something that reads neatly and smoothly will often have the merit of clarity, even though the ideas produced by the writer may be relatively pedestrian. Conversely, an essay will fail to impress despite many potentially perceptive thoughts, if it is so involved and confused that those who read it cannot find their way through it. Thus, the way the essay is structured is just as important as its thought content.

There are several types of structure you may use as a vehicle for your ideas.

1   THE STRONG STRUCTURE

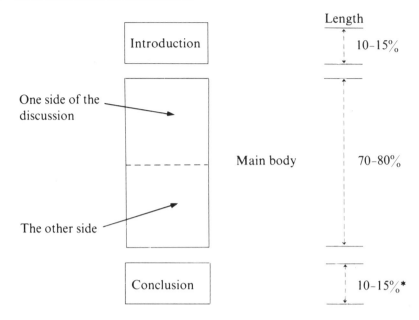

The above diagram is a simple and effective model on which to base the structuring of your essay. It is suitable for many different types of essay topic, since it is straightforward enough to be flexible. If followed closely, it disciplines the essay-writer into a logical approach. The composition is written in three distinct and recognizable sections: an introduction, a main body and a conclusion. Within the argument, the points for either side are kept separate and the stages of development within the essay are signalled to the reader in a series of clear and identifiable steps.

Additionally, if you become accustomed to following such a structure, you will find yourself automatically prepared for the *shape* of your composition, even before you begin writing it. As one of the major problems confronting the essay-writer is often the *shape* of what is being written, such preparation can only be beneficial, especially in the examination situation when the proper organization of available time is so important.

The crux of this structure is the recognition that many types of essay topic, despite their apparent difference, require the writer to discuss two sides of a question and to reach some sort of conclusion as to which side is the stronger. Hence the name, the *strong* structure. If you can break an essay-title down into a requirement for a two-sided discussion and hold back the side which you favour until the second half of your thesis, then you will have created a *strong* position from which to influence the reader.

When the reader reaches the conclusion of the essay, most of what is upper-

*Less in a lengthy essay.

most in his or her mind will relate to the points most recently read. Presented with a considerable amount of information to read, the human mind quite naturally recalls best what it has just processed. Thus, if you, the writer, are attempting to sway the reader towards those arguments you favour, it is advisable to leave these points until the later stages of your composition.

A major difficulty often experienced in writing essays is the fact that it is not always possible to feel very positively about one side of the question. You may feel sufficiently interested in a topic to want to write about it, but your views on the subject may be very mixed. This need not deter you from using an extension of the strong structure, in which you still divide the main body of the essay into two distinct halves but end with no firm commitment to the superiority of one side of the argument.

Suitable topics for the strong structure

Here are some examples of essay topics for which you may use the strong structure, despite their apparent lack of common ground:

(a) A's plays are intrinsically theatrical and do not lend themselves to literary study.
(b) How far do you agree with the statement that X theme is a key to the understanding of Y's work?
(c) What makes B a credible character in C's work?

In (a) you would decide how much of a purely theatrical quality there was in the plays and what exactly there was in the way of literary merit. You would then have to try to decide which took precedence.

Example (b) is perhaps the simplest type of two-sided observation. You decide the extent of your agreement, find what points you can to support each side and order the two sides accordingly. If there is little you can find to support one side of the statement, then the main body of your essay must be one-sided.

Example (c) This is a common type of essay-question, in which you would be well advised not to fall into the trap of absolute agreement. The character will undoubtedly be highly credible, otherwise the title would not have been devised. However, every author is capable of lapses. Check through the text to see if you can find examples of these. There will probably not be many. Still, one or two such instances at the beginning of the main body, will show the reader your astuteness. The points you then make in support of the title will have the weight of authority behind them.

2 THE CHRONOLOGICAL STRUCTURE

This structure is used with essay topics in which you are required to trace a sequence of events or of significant stages. Using a structure in which you list points in the order in which they occur, you will produce an essay which looks something like this:

```
┌─────────────────────────────────┐
│ INTRODUCTION                    │
└─────────────────────────────────┘

┌─────────────────────────────────┐
│ EVENT/CHANGE/STAGE   A          │
└─────────────────────────────────┘
┌─────────────────────────────────┐
│ EVENT/CHANGE/STAGE   B          │
└─────────────────────────────────┘
┌─────────────────────────────────┐
│ EVENT/CHANGE/STAGE   C          │
└─────────────────────────────────┘
┌─────────────────────────────────┐
│ EVENT/CHANGE/STAGE   D          │
└─────────────────────────────────┘
┌─────────────────────────────────┐
│ EVENT/CHANGE/STAGE   E          │
└─────────────────────────────────┘

┌─────────────────────────────────┐
│ CONCLUSION                      │
└─────────────────────────────────┘
```

Chronological topics read like the examples below:

(a) Trace the development of the character of Rustan in *Der Traum ein Leben*.
(b) Analyse the stages leading to Woyzeck's demise in Büchner's masterpiece.
(c) From your reading of Wedekind's short stories, show how his technique can be said to have matured.

Note the key-words *development, stages leading, matured*. They indicate the need to take your points in chronological sequence.

3 THE ROLLING STRUCTURE

This is basically the same type of structure as (2), with the difference that you are not required to take items chronologically. Points A–E (or F) are separate and may roll or flow into each other, but, here, you have the freedom to move as you like within the sequence of the work.

INTRODUCTION

DEVICE/THEME/ITEM   A

DEVICE/THEME/ITEM   B

DEVICE/THEME/ITEM   C

DEVICE/THEME/ITEM   D

DEVICE/THEME/ITEM   E

DEVICE/THEME/ITEM   F

DEVICE/THEME/ITEM   G

DEVICE/THEME/ITEM   H

CONCLUSION

Types of topic which fit this pattern are:

(a) What devices does Böll use to achieve a tense effect in *Und sagte kein einziges Wort?*
(b) What is the basic theme in Dürrenmatt? (Or, analyse the main themes recurrent in the work of Dürrenmatt.)
(c) Trace the historical inaccuracies in *Maria Stuart.*

4 THE CONTRASTIVE STRUCTURE

Topics in this category are of the *compare and contrast* type, such as:

(a) Compare Brecht and Zuckmayer's treatment of the theme of the State in their plays.
(b) In what ways may George and Trakl both be said to be poets of their time?
(c) Compare and contrast the characters of Tell and Gessler in *Wilhelm Tell.*

Although you may not find it hard to obtain sufficient material to enable you to write on such topics, *contrastives* are a trap for the inexperienced, as the diagram of a typical contrastive essay below will show.

INTRODUCTION

A's quality/reaction/device/attitude, etc.
↕   **compared with**   ↕
B's quality/reaction/device/attitude, etc.

A's quality/reaction/device/attitude, etc.
↕   **compared with**   ↕
B's quality/reaction/device/attitude, etc.

A's quality/reaction/device/attitude, etc.
↕   **compared with**   ↕
B's quality/reaction/device/attitude, etc.

A's quality/reaction/device/attitude, etc.
↕   **compared with**   ↕
B's quality/reaction/device/attitude, etc.

CONCLUSION

In this type of essay, you are always moving backwards and forwards between A and B, and so you will need to write in a particularly clear and succinct manner to avoid confusing the reader. You may find it easier to use a form of the *strong structure*, i.e. to discuss the various facets of A in the first part of the main-body and then to do the same for B, remarking on the contrasts and comparisons with A as they arise.

THE INTRODUCTION AND THE CONCLUSION

These sections are, of course, common to all the various structures we have looked at, but should not be overlooked simply because they are obvious parts of any essay. Their own internal structures merit as much analysis as the main body.

THE INTRODUCTION

This initial section (of one or two paragraphs and approximately 10–15 per cent of the total length of the essay) should be exactly what its name implies: it should introduce the reader to the theme. Avoid the temptation to start with a collection of vague sentences which have little to do with the topic.

What steps should you take to ensure that the introduction is direct, relevant and interesting? If the following points can be answered positively, then as far as the thought-content and ideas are concerned, your reader's first reaction is likely to be favourable.

Have you:

1 *made at least an oblique reference to the title?* A partial allusion to the title helps to tie you to your theme. It is worth reminding yourself that digression irritates the majority of readers. But there is no need to repeat it exactly. A paraphrase or the use of part of the actual title will suffice. Precise repetition, particularly if it occurs several times, suggests that you lack the ability to express the idea yourself.

2 *presented a list of the main points to come?* The introduction is often at its most effective when it draws together the main points to be dealt with in the main body of the essay. It tends to have a direct quality, prepares the reader for what is to come, and helps to check the writer's natural tendency to wander from his plan. It has the further advantage of imparting a logical feel to the assignment, when the reader can see that what is promised in the introduction actually occurs in the following paragraphs. All too often, there is little connection between introduction and main body, so that, by contrast, such a start creates an impression of a clear and organized mind.

3 *given some indication of your personal stance?* Somewhere in the introduction, you should give the reader an indication of your particular standpoint. This does not need to be too forceful or to follow the *it is my belief that/I am of the opinion that* pattern; it may be put much less personally.

4 *provided a smooth lead-in to the main body?* If the above suggestions have been followed, then the introduction is likely to have provided a smooth lead into the main body, since the first main point with which one is about to deal, will already have been briefly mentioned. Should there seem to you to be a hiatus between the introduction and the main section, then there may well have been a lack of relevance, clarity or direction in the first paragraph(s). Indeed, a careful look at the junction point between sections 1 and 2 of the essay is a useful check, since you will be able to tell by the smooth or jerky transition, whether or not the introduction has done its job.

5 *left room for manoeuvre in the conclusion?* Avoid the temptation to list every main idea in the introduction or you may be left with nothing new to say in the conclusion. As you will note in the next section, there is a considerable tendency for the conclusion to be a barely disguised regurgitation of the introduction. Thus, it is advisable to leave one important point to be made at the end of the essay, so that it does not simply peter out.

6 *avoided making your introduction too long/too short?* It is the introduction which gives your readers their first impressions of the worth of your ideas. Too long an introduction is likely to wander from the point, to be too comprehensive, or at worst mere padding. Too short an introduction will look thin and inadequate. Ideally, the first few sentences should be a succession of clearly expressed statements which are relevant to the title and give some indication of your personal assessment.

THE CONCLUSION

As has already been pointed out, many otherwise well-written compositions lose some credit in the very last lines, because the conclusion is almost an exact repetition of the introduction. This tendency to reproduce the opening stages of the essay in the final paragraph can be countered in a variety of ways. It may help, for instance, if you can write the end without looking back at the beginning. This is by no means foolproof, however, since ideas from the introduction are likely to resurface in the mind, when you come to concentrate on the conclusion.

If, however, you can select a specific style of closure, which is quite different from the way you led into the main body, this will avoid the danger of repetition.

STANDARD APPROACHES FOR INTRODUCTIONS AND CONCLUSIONS

(a) Agreeing or disagreeing with the title

Either at the beginning or the end of your essay you will have to give some indication of where you stand on the issue(s) raised. As has previously been suggested, it is not necessary to make your statement into a personal credo. As the central idea in your final paragraph(s), simply state *what the author has or has not succeeded in doing/how far such-and-such a critic's objection is justified, etc.* Below are examples of what we might call *'kernel' introductory or concluding statements*:

> *Sansibar oder der letzte Grund* is a fast-moving novel of escape. It has a dramatic tension which is maintained at almost every stage of the story and it presents a very genuine evocation of the atmosphere of fear and suspicion pervading a Baltic fishing town a short time before the outbreak of the Second World War. But, it is much more than an interesting tale of escape, since its underlying concern is with human values and with what can be achieved by the spirit, when people of goodwill are prepared to come together and co-operate in the name of goodness and decency.

> We have seen that the critic's objection to Brecht's plays as little more than method-writing produced by a propagandist can only have any real relevance to the *Lehrstücke*. Bertolt Brecht's best work is one of the major achievements of twentieth century drama, bringing together, as it does, colour, warmth, passion, movement and an inspiring commitment to humanity.

(b) Taking the middle position

You may not necessarily be in complete agreement or disagreement with the question. In such a case, it is perfectly appropriate for you to occupy the middle ground, as in this example:

> Dürrenmatt's detective novels are only works of detection in a relatively limited sense, since the author's main preoccupation is with the implications of the conflict between Bärlach and Gastmann, as symbolical representations of the forces of Good and Evil. Nonetheless, Dürrenmatt succeeds in maintaining a tension, and the answers to certain

key questions are left until the end of the works, in the best traditions of the detective genre.

(c) Coming to a relative assessment
Often the question itself will not expect you to take up a polarized position, in which case your conclusion may include a drawing together of the threads along the lines of (b). Essay questions of this type look like the following:

In what sense may Böll's *Wo warst du, Adam?* be regarded as pure 'Trümmerliteratur'?
How fully may Anna Seghers be regarded as a *communist* writer?
To what extent is Eichendorff's *Taugenichts* a credible character?
How far are Georg Kaiser's expressionist works relevant to our modern society?

(d) Using the author (or critic)'s own statement
If you have read the background to a work you are studying sufficiently well, a quotation from it will often provide the basis for your summing-up:

When Günter Grass wrote in his poem *Kleckerburg*, 'Und aufgewachsen bin ich zwischen dem Heilgen Geist und Hitlers Bild', he provided the reader with a clear statement of two of the major influences on much of his work. His relationship with the Roman Catholic Church and his training in the Hitler youth movement combine to provide an abiding feeling of guilt at the actions that a whole generation of which he was part was obliged to perpetrate.

(e) Starting with a quotation
Similarly to (d), a quotation from the author or a close contemporary may set the tone for the whole of your conclusion:

'Gleich mit seinem ersten Roman, *Mutmaßungen über Jakob*, ist er zum Dichter der beiden Deutschland geworden.' Günter Blöcker's admiration for Uwe Johnson is unequivocal and the general reader shares the critic's belief that Johnson provides an eloquent and lyrical statement of the two-german-ness. The basic question we ask ourselves when reading *Mutmaßungen* is, 'Who was this certain Jakob Abs, who no longer had a home in the East and remained a stranger in the West?'

(f) Giving a short historical background
An allusion to the background of the author or of the work will often help to set the final point that you are making:

Draussen vor der Tür was conditioned by Wolfgang Borchert's experiences as a soldier while still a late teenager, as a prisoner under sentence of death for writing letters criticising Hitler and, once pardoned, as a prisoner again, for having joked about the Third Reich. It is hardly surprising that his play contains such a clear message for those of us who survive war. We should not be taken in by 'das törichte Pathos der Fahnen, das Geknalle der Salutschüsse und der fade Heroismus der Trauermärsche.'

DRAWING UP A PLAN

Always follow a regular sequence of steps, such as these:

1 Write the title at the top of your sheet.
2 Look through the margin-notes in your text-book and/or your quote-book (see pages 37–9).
3 Make a list of 6–8 brief points to form the main body, together with page references for quotes.
4 Sketch out the Intro. Para. as a form of introductory list of these points.
5 Sketch out a Concluding Para.
6 Note any relevant external quotes or parallels in lit./films/music/radio/ theatre, etc.
7 Start writing the essay, referring whenever necessary to your plan.
8 Every time you start a new paragraph, look at your title.

CHECKLIST

When you have finished writing your essay, devise a checklist such as the one below, to help you see where improvements might have been made. If the answer to several of these questions is *no*, then you should try to amend the essay, time permitting.

COMPLETED ESSAY CHECK-LIST

Have I ...?
  the right length?
  sufficient main-points?
  sufficient quotes?
  checked their accuracy?
  both a definite Intro. + Concln.?
  made outside reference?
  the right balance of arguments?
  looked for padding?
  looked for repetition?
  kept on theme?
  ended on a positive note?

Look through any literature essays you have written before studying this chapter. Use the checklist to help you see how you might have improved these essays.

ASSIGNMENTS

Draw up plans for the following essay topics: Instead of producing a full plan, you may find it a useful exercise, simply to write out a list of textual references and/or quotes, which cover the points you would make.

Section A (using the strong structure)
1 If you are studying a play, in which ways does it lend itself to literary study and which of its theatrical qualities are likely to escape the reader?
2 Choose one of your German authors and decide how far you agree with the statement that a knowledge of his/her background is essential to an understanding of his/her work.
3 Choose a character from one of your texts and show in which ways (s)he arouses both sympathy and irritation in the reader.

Section B (using the chronological structure)
4 Take one of your set texts and trace the development of a character of your choice.
5 Analyse the stages leading to the success or downfall of a character or strategy in a text you have studied.
6 From the reading of one of your German authors' novels/short stories/poetry, to what extent would you say his/her outlook changes throughout his/her work?

Section C (using the rolling structure)
7 What are the typical devices used by your favourite German author?
8 Analyse the main themes present in one of your texts.
9 If you have studied a German text based on historical fact, show how (in) accurate it has been in its treatment of events.

Section D (using the contrastive structure)
10 Compare and contrast two (main) characters in any work of German literature you have read.

Section E General assignments
11 Look at the Past Paper-type essay questions on page 117 in Appendix 4 and label each one A, B, C, or D, according to which type of structure best suits it.
12 Look at pages 121–3 and list all the essays best suited to the contrastive structure.
13 For each of the German set books you have studied, produce your own list of the sort of questions you might expect at A-level. Label each one A-D, according to its type.

4

The use of quotations

Many people avoid direct quotation when they write a literature essay. Others pepper their essay with so many lengthy quotations that the finished product seems to be little more than extracts from the work under discussion, strung together by the odd sentence.

The answer is of course the happy medium between these two extremes. It will be an essay which is fundamentally an analysis by yourself of the work in relation to your title theme, illustrated by suitable quotations of the right length. This is fine and pious advice, but how is such a happy medium achieved? The following pointers will help you:

A   PUNCTUATION

The selected passage should always be given between quotation marks. If it is indented from the margin, it will look neat and will stand out.

B   THE LENGTH OF THE QUOTATION

In general, and with few exceptions, this should be 1–5 lines. In order to keep within these limits, dots may be used within the passage quoted to allow you to omit unnecessary material, as in the example below:

> 'Ich bin nicht Stiller. Was wollen Sie von mir! Ich bin ein unglücklicher, nichtiger, unwesentlicher Mensch, der kein Leben hinter sich hat, überhaupt keines. Wozu mein Geflunker? Nur damit sie mir meine Leere lassen, meine Nichtigkeit, meine Wirklichkeit, denn es gibt keine Flucht, und was sie mir anbieten, ist Flucht, nicht Freiheit, Flucht in eine Rolle. Warum lassen sie nicht ab?'

> 'Ich bin nicht Stiller. Was wollen sie von mir! Ich bin ein unglücklicher, nichtiger, unwesentlicher Mensch, der kein Leben hinter sich hat, überhaupt keines . . . was sie mir anbieten, ist Flucht, nicht Freiheit, Flucht in eine Rolle. Warum lassen sie nicht ab?'

> Max Frisch: *Stiller*

The person producing the quotation in its condensed form is making the point that for the American called White, who has been mistaken for a Zürich sculptor by the name of Stiller, to opt out of his present difficulties by accepting this new identity is not a solution. It is merely an escape into playing a false part. Two lines have been removed, since the rest of the material is sufficient for the point to be effective. Notice how condensation makes the point sharper.

C SETTING OUT THE QUOTATION

If the quote is less than a line, it may be most easily worked into a sentence in your own paragraphs:

> When one reads that for Ellen, 'der Preis für die Torte war der Stern', one wonders what similar experiences Ilse Aichinger and her family underwent during the German occupation of Austria.

As suggested in A, quotations of more than one line are better separated from the paragraph containing your argument and given their own independent position on the line below:

> Hofmannsthal's preoccupation with the need of the immature aesthete, who is in a state of 'Prä-existenz', to accept the challenge of life and to re-immerse himself in the life-stream finds a convenient mouthpiece in Claudio in *Der Tor und der Tod*:
>> 'Jetzt fühl ich – laß mich – daß ich leben kann!
>> Ich fühls an diesem grenzenlosen Drängen:
>> Ich kann mein Herz an Erdendinge hängen'.
>
> Claudio, sensing that death has come to take him, begins to realize quite dramatically the foolishness of an existence in which aestheticism becomes a substitute for real living. But, it is too late!

D COMMENTING ON THE QUOTATION

Teachers and examiners are frequently struck by the failure of great numbers of students to make any sort of comment on the quotations they include. While the significance of certain quotes may be self-evident from the preceding essay paragraph, others, as in the previous example, will be more effective, if they are followed by a short comment, to explain them or to tie them in to the fabric of the essay.

E THE NUMBER OF QUOTATIONS

To a large extent this is a matter of personal choice. As a rule of thumb, the amount of material quoted should not exceed one quarter of the total length of the essay. For example, an open essay occupying four hand-written sides of A4 paper would normally be expected to contain 25–35 lines of quotation. In exam conditions you would do well to include at least 10 per cent of quotation.

F A QUOTE-BOOK

If you are to use your important quotations effectively, they are best kept separate from the rest of your literature notes in a quote-book, which may be kept rather like a vocabulary book. When you are studying a text either with a teacher or on your own, note down the more significant lines, keeping to the sort of maximum length already suggested, and classifying them according to characters or themes. Write in the margin the number of the text-book page on which the quotation occurs, so that you can refer back to it to refresh yourself as to the exact context, etc.

G   LEARNING QUOTES

It is not absolutely necessary to be able to quote verbatim from a text in an examination question, but it is difficult to score high marks without doing so, since your own accuracy of recall will undoubtedly influence how clearly you remember the basic points in the argument you are putting forward.

If you have kept a quote-book, it will obviously be much easier for you to get down to the task of learning lines exactly, since you will already have an organized collection in front of you. Yet, there is still the question of how much you should learn for a particular book. It is difficult to provide a rule of thumb, since some people learn lines much more easily than others. However, working from the basic assumption that examinees are busy people with a great deal of other material to assimilate beside literary quotations, 40–60 lines per book should be an appropriate minimum to allow you to do well.

Of course, although this amount will often take quite a long time to learn, it will frequently represent no more than a very small fraction of the work being studied, so you will have to choose the quotations you are going to learn carefully, since they need to be representative of the book as a whole, i.e. if there are five or six types of theme likely to be encountered as exam questions, make sure you have quotations for every area.

This is not always as difficult as it sounds, since important individual quotations will often be relevant to several themes within the work. A short but good example of this is the quotation from *Der Tor und der Tod*, above. It can be used to highlight a comment on the fin-de-siècle mood in Hofmannsthal's Vienna, or to show that Claudio has at last realised the implications of his situation and of how he has wasted his life. Alternatively, it may simply be used to illustrate a comment on the lyrical style of the *Kleine Dramen*.

Your quote-book will be of considerable help in the tedious task of rote-learning, since, instead of having to look through the whole 60–500 pages of a text, you will find what you want arranged neatly in 5–10 pages of your own notebook, classified under clear headings.

H   TEXT-BOOK NOTATION

This is an erudite term for what is often regarded as the cardinal sin of pencilling in notes in the margin of your text-book. If your teacher has no objection to your marking in pencil in the margin or on the page of your book, you will find this helps you greatly to highlight the important lines on a page. The use of a system such as the one exampled below, allows you to organize a large amount of potentially quotable material in addition to that kept in your notebook:

+ Knudsen's
other side.
His basic
preoccupation,
to look after
mentally ill
wife.
Ich habe es mir hundertmal überlegt, dachte Knudsen. Ich kann ⎫
nicht. Ich kann es Bertha nicht antun. Niemand würde sich um ⎪ a Caring
Bertha kümmern, wenn ich fort wäre. Ich kann sie nicht im Stich ⎬ man
lassen. ⎭

K. is much more than just the surly old fisherman he seems
to be to Helunder and Gregor.

I COMPILING QUOTATIONS FOR ESSAYS

One of the excellent advantages of organizing quotations along the lines
suggested above, is the fact that, because you have classified small but crucial
pieces of text so clearly, you now have a system which will help you to draw up an
essay plan very quickly. Your notebook and marginal notation become a type of
filing cabinet. More often than not, you can construct a plan for a given topic
simply by reference to quotable passages, as in the example:

Theme: What evidence is there in *Kleider machen Leute* to support the view that
Gottfried Keller is a master of irony?
Page no.
24 und ihm sein ehrwürdiger Mantel dienstfertig abgenommen wurde.
25 "Und der junge Mann mag kaum den Mund öffnen vor Vornehmheit!"
26 so glaubte der Kellner . . . jener suche eine gewisse Bequemlichkeit.
39 ein verwachsenes Gerippe erstreckte sich von unten bis oben zwischen den
Fenstern; hier wohnte der Friedensrichter.
46 Ihr vorderster Schlitten mit der Fortuna trug die Inschrift: 'Leute machen
Kleider'.

J REVISION FOR EXAMS

When exam time looms, you are likely to be short of time. It will be unusual for
you to have sufficient at your disposal to allow you to re-read all the texts before
you enter the exam room.

A few hours spent looking through your marginal notes and renewing your
memory of crucial questions will sometimes be enough to give you a fresh and
clear picture of an individual book, if you have read it thoroughly on previous
occasions. Indeed, there is a particular advantage to this approach. Since you do
not have the time to re-read all of the book and are obliged to concentrate on an
important digest of the material, your view of the text is often clearer, because it is
not cluttered by the whole weight of the work.

Efficient exam revision is a logical and relatively painless consequence of the
points discussed above, especially F–I. If you have learnt a reasonable number of
quotations from a book and you have kept them short, they will frequently
resurface in your mind under examination conditions. You need to discipline
yourself to use only those quotations which are appropriate to the theme and to
use them in a correct sequence, much as you would do when compiling quotes for
an essay as in I.

K   PRESS ARTICLES

Many examiners feel it is counterproductive for a student to produce much in the way of reference to this or that critic's view, since what is required is the student's reaction to the book, not a regurgitation or direct quotation of what eminent literati have felt about it.

However, new material referring to authors, their works and background may often appear in the press, especially in papers such as the *Times*, or *Sunday Times*, *The Guardian*, *The Observer*, the *Sunday Telegraph*, and the *Financial Times* or *Radio Times*. The *occasional* quotation from these sources will show initiative on your part. But you would do well to remember to avoid producing an essay full of remarks such as 'Kenneth Tynan said that . . .', 'It was Hermann Glaser's belief that . . .', unless you are going to qualify their observations in some way. It is *your* views that the examiner wishes to read.

5

Reading essay titles correctly

Unfortunately, it is easy to lose yourself much credit by misleading essay titles. In many cases you will not have spent enough time and care over the implications of the title. In others, an already demanding task will have been made more difficult by question compilers who seem to delight in setting complex quotations as a basis for an essay topic. Happily, literature papers are becoming far less of a maze than they used to be, since many examiners now take the view, rightly, that straightforward questions are sufficient to allow a Board to differentiate between candidates and to provide a fair assessment of their abilities.

However, you are still likely to come across at least one or two topics on your paper which will need a considerable amount of unravelling. Let us start with the most daunting type.

COMPLEX QUOTATIONS IN GERMAN

Essay titles based on quotations in German (or English) are the most difficult to treat, since, unlike a straightforward question in English, they often require you to involve yourself in a considerable amount of interpretation, before you can decide exactly what it is you are expected to comment upon. Thus, you run the very clear risk of quite literally misinterpreting the meaning of the quote and of writing an essay on a topic which may be at best unintended and at worst in no way relevant to the work under consideration.

The quotation and the accompanying question may be straightforward enough, as in:

> *What light does Tonio Kröger's question 'Ist der Künstler überhaupt ein Mann?' throw on Thomas Mann's own view of the artist in society?*

However, the statement may be much more complex, as in the following example which is very similar to a question set by one of the Boards:

> *'Schiller hatte die autonome Würde des Menschen in den tragischen Zwiespalt von Natur und Geist gestellt.' (Joachim Müller) Comment on this assessment of Schiller's dramatic opus.*

Here you have four elements to deal with: *autonome Würde/den tragischen Zwiespalt/Natur/Geist*. To add to your difficulties, they are not simply isolated elements. The last three are supposed to be components of the first. Additionally, before you finish the question, you will have to define 'den tragischen Zwiespalt' in terms of Schiller's drama, if you are to understand the implications of your theme.

Many teachers and examiners feel that this type of question is unfair, since it places excessive burdens on the candidate. A complex quotation runs the risk of actually encouraging the candidate to follow a false trail. Fortunately, many Boards now recognize this and there is a discernible tendency towards more straightforward questions. Even those Boards who do indulge in complex quotations still include a large number of more basic questions, the meaning of which may easily be seen, provided you have studied the work reasonably thoroughly.

If you find yourself attempting a question which is a complex quotation, there is something concrete and practical you can do, to help to isolate all the elements. It is a simple device and it will do no more than separate the individual areas to which you must give your attention. The rest will be up to you, but, at least, you will know clearly what you are supposed to be writing about.

The device is called *base and bricks*. It relies on the fact that most complex titles present several sub-themes, all contributing to the main theme, as in the Gide quotation above. If you can visualize the writing of an essay on a complex topic as the building of a small wall with a concrete base, you can represent it diagrammatically in a very simple way:

```
THEME—3
```

```
THEME—2
```

```
THEME—1
```

```
UNIFYING POINT
OR THEME
```

Every time you are confronted with a complex quotation, separate it into the base and the courses above, the base being the main, unifying point. Each course of bricks is one of the principal themes contributing to it. Thus, the daunting quotation with which you have just been presented:

Schiller hatte die autonome Würde des Menschen in dem tragischen Zwiespalt von Natur und Geist gestellt.

can be alleviated once you have established its structure:

```
nature
```

```
the intellect
```

```
tragic conflict
```

```
independent worth
```

The metaphor of the wall to be built is an appropriate one. You must first work out your base, before you build your essay. You will, of course, add an extra course for each additional theme. If you usually have trouble organizing examples of each theme when you write an essay, you could make each brick into a specific reference to the text.

'ORDINARY' ESSAY TITLES

Having accepted that difficult or lengthy titles need close concentration, you must not forget that straightforward, brief topics need their own form of attention.

Questions such as:

Discuss the role of X in Y.
Compare and contrast the characters of A and B in C.
How far is D's attitude a reflection of E's own position?

for all their apparent simplicity, are not candidate-proof. That is, they cannot guarantee that you will produce the right material dealing with the right area of the work.

Discuss the | *role* | *of X* can easily be interpreted as *Discuss the* | character | *of X*, if you have a mind to, especially if you have not thought about what the character *does* in the work and why.

Similarly, *Compare and contrast the characters of A and B* may easily deteriorate into *Write notes on the characters of A and B*, without any effort to *compare and contrast* the qualities and behaviour of the two individuals.

Some examination candidates actually go as far as completely ignoring one character or the other, either through lack of textual knowledge, or because they find one easier to write on than the other. It is impossible for them to obtain a pass-mark for such an answer.

Undoubtedly, there is often a tendency, especially in exam conditions, for some candidates to succumb to what one might term a *latch-on* effect. That is, for reasons of over- or of under-confidence, they skim through a title and *latch-on* to a few words, which they construe as they want. Thus, the third example question above becomes:

Give a summary of D's attitude

which, once more, is not at all what is being asked.

Whenever you have to choose a literary essay topic, look closely at key words like:

role/contrast/compare/significance/analyse/assess/function/purpose

and treat them with proper respect.

AGREEING WITH THE QUESTION

Naturally, when you have gone to the trouble of studying and entering for an exam, you want to pass it. Because of this simple fact, you may suffer from a very understandable tendency to try to ingratiate yourself with your examiners or teachers by agreeing with everything in the essay title in front of you. This is especially true in *How far . . .?* questions:

> How far do you feel Judith in *Sansibar oder der letzte Grund* to be a credible character?
> To what extent may *Der Richter und sein Henker* be termed a detective novel?
> How fair would it be to regard Heinrich Böll's *Wo warst du, Adam?* as a dated novel of the immediate postwar period?

The key to your reaction actually lies in the *qualified* nature of the questions *How far . . .?* and *To what extent . . .?* With any or all three of the sample questions, you might or might not be expected to be in *qualified* agreement with the underlying point. But this means that there will be some divergences. There will be some implications of the work for which the comment is not valid and you should try to provide a balanced assessment. You should show where the judgement is correct and where it is not so.

Always be on the lookout for questions where you do not have to be in total agreement with the main point of the title.

6

Character analysis

Both during your A-level course and in the actual examination, you will be presented with essay questions relating to individual characters, their development, their function or role within a work, the author's attitude to them, and their inter-relationship with other characters or elements.

In most novels, short stories and plays, and in some poetry, the characters and the way they behave and grow will be central to an understanding of the work and of the author's purpose. Why is this?

In some ways, a prose work is like a photograph album. Imagine an album filled with photographs of land-, sea- and town-scapes, where the photographer has decided to take a group of pictures containing no interesting people. Most of us would react to the album in a fairly predictable manner. Yes, a pleasant series of pretty pictures, but they are somehow incomplete. It is the people and animals who inhabit these places who give them much of their meaning, since our life is a combination of the places in which we find ourselves and the people with whom we have contact.

Thus, a successful writer must have some ability to produce characters and to flesh them out, so that they come alive and interact in a way that contributes something to the central purpose of the work.

Your task is to assess just how successful the author has been in producing characters who are credible and who fulfil the role for which they were intended.

To do this, you need to analyse your own reactions, as well as those of the personality under your microscope. This means you will often have to walk something of a tightrope. It may be good for you to react strongly to fictional people, but it will not be good if your emotions are so strong that you lose the ability to treat them rationally.

For example, you may find a character to be petty, soulless, aggressive and conceited. Your next step is not to feel particularly hostile to him every time he crops up in the work, but, rather, to ask yourself the following questions:

(a) Am I meant to see this person as such an unpleasant individual, or am I reading into the text things which are not there?
(b) If I am intended to react as I have done, what is the author's purpose?

THE AUTHOR'S PURPOSE

The character will not have arrived in the work by accident. In the real world, all types of people will move in and out of our lives randomly, but, because a novel or a play is a fictionalized and nearly always condensed slice of life, virtually all its people will have been included to some purpose. A writer simply cannot afford the space to allow a variety of incidental characters to stroll through the pages of the work. Therefore any person who appears more than fleetingly has to earn his or her keep.

This state of affairs will actually help you in writing essays, since you can be sure that almost all characters will have some significance. Your first task may be to determine just what this significance is. Most important characters are likely to fulfil one or more of the following roles.

THE AUTHOR'S MAIN CONCERN

A person under emotional, psychological or environmental stress/a maturing or deteriorating individual/a mirror of the age or of social conditions/an object lesson.

A CATALYST

A device to help the action along or to precipitate a situation. In Alfred Andersch's *Sansibar oder der letzte Grund*, for example, 'der lesende Klosterschüler' may be referred to as a catalyst, since he provokes a variety of different people first into conflict and then into positive co-operation.

Sometimes the function of an individual in a story will be particularly obvious, but before you make any attempt to determine his role, it will pay dividends to look at his character. Clearly, if you know well what sort of a person you are dealing with, you will be in a better position to say exactly why that person has a place in the work.

PERSONALITY

It is not always as easy to assess the personality of a character in fiction as it is that of someone you know in real life. The reason for this is very basic. A book gives you less to go on than months or years of frequent exposure to a real person. So, in a book you will have to look more carefully and make good use of the smaller amounts of information given to you.

However, you *will* have the advantage that the author will often state quite categorically several of a person's traits. Nevertheless, deciding what someone's character is like is not particularly easy, even in the real situation.

Most people tend to make value-judgements about people on a snap basis; for instance, if they have been especially sly or helpful towards us on one or two occasions, then they are assumed to be generally cunning or amiable. For the most part, you will tend to categorize people as nice or not nice, friendly or unfriendly, without going into every single reason why. Yet, when you analyse a character in a book, you are expected to produce an accurate and balanced assessment.

INDIVIDUAL TRAITS AND A CHARACTER-PROFILE

Picking over the bones of a fictional person's character, then, is not easy, but it should not prove impossible. Look at the character-profile on page 48 and you will see a long list of individual qualities. Before trying to pick out specific traits belonging to a figure in one of your set texts, you will find it helpful to assess the broad basis of the persona.

Instead of starting, for example, by wondering whether (s)he is sympathetic/conceited/tragic/neurotic, etc., ask yourself:

Is this person generally a positive or a negative individual?
Is there a side of his/her character which clashes with the general picture he/she presents?
Is my reaction to him/her sympathetic or not?
What are his/her two or three most striking characteristics?

If you follow this procedure, your analysis will probably develop along the following lines:

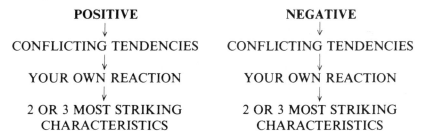

POSITIVE	NEGATIVE
↓	↓
CONFLICTING TENDENCIES	CONFLICTING TENDENCIES
↓	↓
YOUR OWN REACTION	YOUR OWN REACTION
↓	↓
2 OR 3 MOST STRIKING CHARACTERISTICS	2 OR 3 MOST STRIKING CHARACTERISTICS

ASSIGNMENT

The character-profile is explained in detail below. Before using it for literary character-analysis, choose four people whom you know well at home or in school and try to select from the list in the profile *ten* personality traits, which you think fit each of these real people. It may be advisable not to make the results too public, as most people do not like being reminded of their foibles!

CHARACTER PROFILE

From each row, select one or two* adjectives which describe the character under consideration and write them in the box at the side. Score the items in the box on the scale 1–3, e.g.

sympathetic–3; impulsive–1;
indicates the individual is very sympathetic and a little impulsive.

Title of Work: . . . .   *Character:* . . . .
PROFILE BOX

sympathetic conceited tragic neurotic

distant impulsive wise cowardly

weak overbearing carefree resentful

strong comic anxious generous

irrational humanitarian brave prudent

proud violent considerate warm

relaxed mournful magnanimous sinister

compassionate ruthless progressive feckless

aggressive affectionate conservative calm

wary modest demanding scornful

world-weary scolding coarse exuberant

gentle hopeless humorous energetic

despairing cheerful humble morbid

happy hopeful passive insecure

passionate petty forgiving confident

serious pessimistic sad refined

soulless boorish earthy determined

other qualities not listed: . . . .

Notes to be read before completing the profile:

   * Unless it is absolutely necessary do NOT select more than at most two qualities from any one line.

   Do not feel obliged to fill in each line of the box. It is likely that there will be some lines in which none of the qualities fits the character you are examining.

   When you have completed the box, find examples in your text which illustrate each point of character.

N.B. IF a character in the work under study changes considerably during the course of events, complete a profile for him/her as he/she appears on both early and later acquaintance.

USING THE CHARACTER-PROFILE

Each line of the profile contains four qualities or attitudes. Normally, you would not expect to find more than two from a line in any one individual. When you are required to analyse a literary character, work your way through the grid line by line. With each line, decide which (if any) of the traits is/are discernible in the character under examination, write the trait(s) in the profile-box and try to give page references to passages in the text illustrating the point.

When you have completed the profile-box, you are likely to have uncovered a reasonably large number of traits. Now decide which of these are most significant in the character's make-up and in his/her role in the work. Concentrate on these in your essay and bring in the points of lesser significance only if they should prove relevant.

ASSIGNMENT

Take *three* important characters from the German texts you have studied so far and use the profile to help you to draw up a list of their traits. For each character, sum up in 4–5 lines your personal reaction, in as unemotional terms as possible.

CHARACTER DEVELOPMENT

Your task in assessing character is not always simply a question of producing a list of an individual's strengths and weaknesses. Often, a character will show a steady development or major change during the course of the work you are studying. Part of your brief is to note the stages in this change.

Always ask yourself the question, *Are this person's behaviour and attitudes really static or has there been some noticeable change?*

The central point or interest of the work may in fact hinge upon such a change, as in *Sansibar, oder der letzte Grund* where a boy is forced by the coincidence of external events and pressures to grow up quickly enough to be able to accept his responsibilities as a young adult.

A major theme in Gottfried Keller's *Kleider machen Leute* is the development of the young Wenzel into a mature adult, as he comes to accept responsibility for his own actions.

In such a large work as Keller's Bildungsroman, *Der grüne Heinrich*, Heinrich Lee is subject to many influences and events. The changes brought in him are more gradual and take longer to occur. Indeed, the novel ends with his death, but Keller strikes a sanguine note. It is not a time for mourning, other than in the most literal sense:

So ging denn der tote grüne Heinrich auch den Weg hinauf in den alten Kirchhof, wo sein Vater und seine Mutter lagen. Es war ein schöner, freundlicher Sommerabend, als man ihn mit Verwunderung und Teilnahme begrub, und es ist auf seinem Grabe ein recht frisches und grünes Gras gewachsen.

Some, at least, of the last few examples, will have shown you that, frequently, when we look at an individual's character, we have to be concerned with the way it *develops* within the work. Always ask yourself if the separate facets of a character's makeup eventually contribute to a general maturing or decline in the person under examination.

ASSIGNMENTS

1 Choose a main character from one of your set books and, using short quotations, show how his/her character develops or remains static during the course of the work.

2 Select 4–6 example passages in a book you are studying to illustrate any *one* of the following qualities in a character of your choice:

sympathetic/distant/weak/overbearing/comic/tragic/violent/irrational/ impulsive/proud/wise/humanitarian/kind/inadequate/anxious/carefree/ evil

3 Look back at the list of qualities in the Assignment on page 47 and name for each one any character you have encountered who fits the description.

4 Think of an unpleasant character in a set book. Try to locate instances in the text, which show him/her to have redeeming characteristics.

5 Is there any character you have encountered in German literature whose behaviour sometimes seems markedly inconsistent with his/her normal actions? Find example passages in the text to prove your point.

6 Find a character to whom you relate very positively. Give short examples from the text to show why you like him/her.

7 Do the same for a character whom you dislike.

8 Choose a character from a set book, who reminds you of someone you have seen in a film. Make notes on their similarities.

9 Think of a character in real life who resembles one of the characters in a German book you have read. Make notes on their similarities.

10 Can you find a character in a set book who is simply not true to life? Give 4–6 short examples of his/her behaviour to prove your point.

11 Study the behaviour of a character in a set book and describe where it is typically German/Swiss/Austrian.

12 Do you know a work in which any main character resembles the author? Find 3–4 sample passages to support your view.

13 If any main character resembles a famous historical person, find passages in the work which illustrate this similarity.

14 Find 4–6 example passages in which one of your authors uses physical description to convey character.

15 Is there a conflict between the characters of two of the main protagonists in any of the German books that you have read? If so, find 3–5 points of contrast between the two people.

16 Is there a character in any of your set books who is essentially tragic? Draw examples from the text to show exactly what it is which makes the individual tragic.

7

The novel or short-story essay

In some respects it is easier to write an essay about a novel, or a collection of short stories, than to deal with some of the more specialized aspects of drama or of poetry. However, prose narratives have their own technicalities, which you should always bear in mind. Most of these technical points are concerned with the structure of the prose work.

If you learn to look for the elements and devices used by authors in building their finished works, this will help you, not simply to write an essay on, say, the structure of a novel, but, more often, to include general points on composition in essays relating to wider themes. In other words, the structure of the work will almost always be significant in questions on say character, plot, social themes, since the way the book is built up goes a long way towards determining how you react to an individual within the story, or to the concluson of the tale, and so on.

For example, if an author spends a great deal of time building up detail in a painstaking manner, rather in the way that life itself often evolves slowly, then you are likely to see characters within the work as fully-drawn individuals. If another author concentrates on the description of the natural background and spends proportionately less time on the characters, then you will either see the people in the story very much as creations of their environment, or you will gain the impression that the author is less concerned with human beings than with the (natural) world which surrounds them.

Questions on basic structure tend to look like the following:

(a) What elements does . . . use to create a picture of sophisticated life in . . . ?
(b) In what ways . . . be said to be a romantic/naturalistic/surrealist novel?
(c) How far can . . . be said to be the work of an experimentalist?
(d) Which devices does . . . use to maintain the reader's interest throughout the work?
(e) How does . . . maintain the tension/action/story-line throughout the work?
(f) How far does . . . succeed in his/her basic purpose in writing . . . ?

However, other examination questions may focus on structure within a work, as in

(g) What use does the author make of an episodic technique in . . . ?
(h) Why is background so important in . . . ?
(i) What use does the author make of the . . . motif in . . . ?

(j) What part does silence play in . . . ?
(k) What does the author achieve through his use of a cinema flashback technique in . . . ?
(l) Where in . . . does the author depart from his theoretical naturalism?
(m) How successful is the author in the innovations she uses in . . . ?

ASSIGNMENTS

1 Take any of the question-types (a)–(f) above, adapt it to one of your set books and draw up an essay plan, concentrating on the points of structure discussed below.
2 Follow the same procedure with any one question-type from (g) to (m). Remember that you may well have to adapt, so that your title may become something like *Why is the FAMILY so important in . . . ?* or *What part does MUSIC play in . . . ?*, etc.

So that you may be able to analyse the building-blocks of a work of prose narrative, let us look at the basic elements of structure in some detail.

1 THE BASIC NARRATIVE TECHNIQUE

This is the foundation on which the rest of the work will be built. Ask yourself these questions:

Is the narrative smooth-flowing or does the author deliberately hold it up at times?

Does it follow a straightforward chronological sequence or does it adopt an episodic pattern in which the chapters or sections are distinct and deliberately separate?

At the beginning of a new section, does the author go back somewhat in time, to look at a different character's involvement in the action?

Is the narrative divided into neat chapters/sections, or is it one continuous flow?

Do the episodes follow each other in a logical sequence, or does the author keep switching backwards and forwards in time?

What is the purpose of the basic technique?

Is it to involve/distance the reader?

Does it underline the complex relationships between individual lives and events?

Is one made to feel that characters are leading largely separated and isolated/inter-connected lives?

Does the author allow his/her personal attitudes to intrude?

If so, is this achieved by frequent interventions/occasional very direct comments/the placing side-by-side of contrasting situations and events/historical allusions/the use of parables/the inclusion of a great deal of emotive imagery and events?

Does the author take us into his/her confidence or are we kept in suspense? For what reasons?

Is the detail carefully worked out or are there clear flaws in the compilation of the narrative?

Why does the author pay so much attention to detail/appear to disregard the need for accuracy?

2 BACKGROUND

In most cases the backcloth against which the characters play out their roles will have a major effect on the way they are seen. If the author does no more than give a few brief touches of background, then the reader will be obliged to concentrate on the action in which the characters are involved.

At this point, perhaps we should clarify the meaning of the term *background*. The word has wider implications than the past life and circumstances of the person being studied. *Backcloth* may be a helpful word here, since *background* really means the whole of the environment, past and present, surrounding a character.

What are the implications of such a background for the individuals under the literary microscope? What effect has the individual's town/city/country/ sea/foreign/sheltered/lively/crude/sophisticated environment provoked? Is the character a product of that environment? Does (s)he accept it or rebel against it? Is it a background which is accurately portrayed and readily recognized or is it highly artificial?

ASSIGNMENT

Analyse the background in any of your set texts and make a list of those elements which have not been listed in the preceding paragraph.

3 THE USE OF MOTIFS

Often, a novel or series of short stories will contain a motif, a recurring device which may symbolize an aspect of one of the characters, the author's own attitude to the work, etc. In Andersch's *Sansibar oder der letzte Grund*, for example, the wooden sculpture becomes almost a central character and symbolises the freedom of thought which the Nazis are so keen to eliminate:

> Er liest alles, was er will. Weil er alles liest, was er will, sollte er eingesperrt werden. Und deswegen muß er jetzt wohin, wo er lesen kann, soviel er will.

In *Der Richter und sein Henker*, Dürrenmatt employs the device of Bärlach's chronic and eventually mortal stomach complaint, to underline the fragility of the forces of good, in their battle with evil. Bärlach has barely a year to live, in which to see to the demonic Gastmann finished:

> 'Nur noch ein Jahr,' antwortete Hungertobel, setzte sich an der Wand seines Ordinationszimmers auf einen Stuhl und sah hilflos zu Bärlach hinüber, der in der

Mitte des Zimmers stand, in ferner, kalter Einsamkeit, unbeweglich und demütig, vor dessen verlorenem Blick der Arzt nun die Augen senkte.

Each time reference is made to Bärlach's condition, we are reminded of the urgency of his mission.

ASSIGNMENT

Look for a recurring motif in any of your German set books and make a list of the occasions on which it occurs in the text.

4 THE USE OF DIALOGUE

Somehow, the importance of dialogue in a prose work tends to be glossed over. It is almost as if the narrative were the only important thing and the passages of speech were included merely to fill a few gaps. Yet, dialogue is a vital element, since it reveals so much about characters and the way they interact. It may be used in any of the following ways.

A TO GIVE PACE AND VARIETY TO THE TEXT

Basic narrative requires more concentration from the reader than is normally the case with speech. Passages of conversation will often break up the pattern and give the work a lighter touch. If you look at the dialogue in one of your texts, provided it is done well, you will see how people do not talk in paragraphs and in chunks of ten lines or so. Many utterances may be just a few words and they can be highly colloquial without detracting from the author's good style.

The famous East German writer, Christa Wolf, uses a great deal of sympathetic humour in many of her stories, to clothe her observations on the family and other aspects of ordinary life. In this short extract from *Juninachmittag*, the interchange between the adult-narrator and the child who is so interested in newspaper horror stories, has an immediate spontaneity:

'Du liest Zeitung?'
'Natürlich. Aber die besten Sachen nimmt Vater mir weg.
Zum Beispiel: "Leiche des Ehemanns in der Bettlade."'
'Das wolltest du unbedingt lesen?'
'Das wäre spannend gewesen. Hatte die Ehefrau den Ehemann ermordert?'
'Keine Ahnung.'
'Oder, wer hatte ihn im Bettkasten versteckt?'
'Aber ich hab doch diesen Artikel nicht gelesen!'
'Wenn ich groß bin, lese ich all diese Artikel. Mir ist langweilig.'

B TO PROVIDE REALISM

The above extract does more than add a little pace and variety to a tale. It has a whiff of realism about it, which is frequently much more difficult to convey in the narrative prose. There is good reason why this should be so. Not all of us read books, but talk is something we all indulge in, frequently. We are, therefore, very familiar with the nuances of speech. What people say in a novel or short story, provided the author knows what he is about, will have a direct appeal to us. Our impression after eavesdropping on the conversation is that Christa Wolf certainly knows children well. When the child in the extract says that her father censors the best parts of the paper, we identify with what she says. There have been times in all our childhoods, when our best pleasures have been interfered with by parents. When the girl tell us how bored she is at the end of the conversation, we sympathise and remember our own, similar states of boredom. Such identification has been brought about by the skilful way in which Christa Wolf has constructed the dialogue and by her ear for the natural rhythms of speech. It is the immediacy of the dialogue which has reached us.

C TO CONVEY CONFLICT AND TO PROVIDE DRAMATIC TENSION

Dialogue is essentially a catechism, a process of questioning and answering, involving two or more people. It is consequently an ideal means of conveying conflict, be it large or small. In *Die Hostie*, Hans Bender uses dialogue for just such a purpose and to increase dramatically the level of tension. Brigitte, who has lost her powder-compact, has persuaded the narrator to dance with her. Intoxicated by the boogie rhythm, he pulls her close to him and she feels a hard object in his pocket:

> Auch Brigitte tanzte gut. Ihr Gesicht glühte. Ich riß sie an mich.
> 'Was hast du da?'
> 'Wo? Was?'
> Ihre Hand fuhr nach meiner Brusttasche: 'Hier!'
> 'Nichts!'
> 'Gib sie her, du Schuft!'
> 'Was denn, Brigitte, ich weiß ja gar nicht—'
> 'Das ist meine Puderdose, du Schuft, du gemeiner, dreckiger Schuft!'
> Sie wollte die Tasche aufreißen. Der Knopf sprang ab.
> Ich stieß sie weg und drängte zur Tür.

You will have noted for yourself the direct, even forceful quality of the conversation, and the speed with which the situation develops. But, look how the speech also conveys character. Brigitte, we learn, is of a fiery temperament and someone of whom it is not wise to make an enemy. The conflict between this couple contains familiar overtones for us. It comes close to our own confrontations, either in reality or in our blacker dreams. Conversation has its own direct quality.

There are other reasons for using dialogue, such as the need to show the contrast between a character's thoughts and his or her actions, but the three above categories will provide the major justification. Whenever possible, look at the function of conversation in the work you are studying and refer to it in an essay on structure, style, character, themes, etc. It will almost always be relevant to an essay topic.

ASSIGNMENTS

1 Find six examples in any one of your German texts where the author uses dialogue to give pace and variety.
2 Find as many examples as you can in any one of your set books of the author's use of dialogue to provide realism.
3 Look through all your German texts and find two or three examples in each, where dialogue has been employed as a means of conveying conflict.

5 INNOVATION AND EXPERIMENT

One of the more significant aspects of the structure of the work may be the author's use of new techniques, or the borrowing of strategies from other media.

The cinema has proved a source of inspiration for many writers who have used its flashback technique to record vivid impressions. At crucial points in the narrative, the reader will be shot back with the character to an event in the past, before returned to the present narrative.

The spectacular success of the thriller, both in the cinema and as a popular form of fiction, has had a considerable success on serious writers. When you are studying the structure of a novel, look for loose ends which are not picked up till later in the action and for a preponderance of chapters which end on a note of suspense.

ASSIGNMENTS

1 Find any evidence you can of the use of cinema techniques in any of your set texts.
2 Is any of your authors a *method writer*, i.e. someone writing to a set formula and sticking very closely to the tenets of a particular movement? Find six examples from the text to prove the point.
3 Someone who is wholly a method writer is hardly likely to be a great author. If you have answered 2, find six specific examples in the work, where the author escapes the limitations of the structure to good purpose.

8

The drama essay

In some ways it is unfortunate that you should have to write literature essays about drama, since plays are meant to be acted, heard and seen, rather than simply read.

The reason that so many plays are studied as literature is that the language they contain has sufficient meaning and depth to it for the work to be studied as a book. Yet it should never be forgotten that the prime quality in any play is its action, or, at least, the activity that occurs between certain of the characters.

When you actually *see* a play in the theatre, what strikes you most are the colour, movement and dramatic tension. You should not leave these out of consideration when you come to write about a play.

Of course, your basic task may often be to analyse the development of an individual's personality within the work, or the relationship between the characters, or a variety of other factors related to themes such as historical accuracy, the author's purpose, his use of source materials, etc. You will inevitably concentrate on an analysis using the type of method developed on pages 45–56, but if you do not try to *see* the play in your mind's eye, as if you had actually been in the audience, you will not be doing justice to the work. The author, who is not just an author, but a playwright, has to develop the whole of the play, not just the written lines.

A useful, though not complete, analogy would be a comparison with the composer who produces an attractive song. The melody-line is undoubtedly vital to its success, but without a base and various items of orchestration, the tune may never reach its full potential.

As a clear example of the need to bear the theatrical aspects of the work in mind, let us look at one of Bertolt Brecht's most famous plays, *Der kaukasische Kreidekreis*. The peasant girl, Grusche, has been contracted to marry the dying Jussup to save her child from starving. In the well-known deathbed scene, Jussup arises from the (almost) dead. Family and neighbours have been brought in for his leaving of this world and are partaking of refreshments round his bed. You can imagine the reaction when he gets up and starts to harangue his step-mother for spending so much on food for the invited guests:

JUSSUP: Wieviel Kuchen wirst du ihnen noch in den Rachen stopfen? Hab ich einen Geldscheißer? (*Die Schwiegermutter fährt herum und starrt ihn entgeistert an. Er klettert hinter dem Fliegenschleier hervor.*) Haben sie gesagt, der Krieg ist aus?

DIE ERSTE FRAU (*im anderen Raum freundlich zu Grusche*): Hat die junge Frau jemand im Feld?

DER MANN: Da ist eine gute Nachricht, daß sie zurückkommen, wie?

JUSSUP: Glotz nicht. Wo ist die Person, die du mir als Frau aufgehängt hast?

(*Da er keine Antwort erhält, steigt er aus der Bettstatt und geht schwankend, im Hemd, an der Schwiegermutter vorbei, in den andern Raum. Sie folgt ihm zitternd mit dem Kuchenblech.*)

DIE GÄSTE (*erblicken ihn. Sie schreien auf*): Jesus, Maria und Josef! Jussup!

(*Alles steht alarmiert auf, die Frauen drängen zur Tür. Grusche, noch auf den Knieen, dreht den Kopf herum und starrt auf den Bauern.*)

JUSSUP: Totenessen, das könnte euch passen. Hinaus, bevor ich euch hinausprügle.

(*Die Gäste verlassen in Hast das Haus. Jussup düster zu Grusche:*)

Das ist ein Strich durch deine Rechnung, wie?

(*Da sie nichts sagt, dreht er sich um und nimmt einen Maiskuchen vom Blech, das die Schwiegermutter hält.*)

Most producers interpret this scene as high farce. The crudity of Jussup's language sets the tone for a wholly incongruous scene, where, much as certain of the mourners may express wonder at Jussup's rising from the dead, the audience is consumed with laughter. The intent is to avoid strong pathos through extreme humour.

The dialogue itself contains enough to amuse the audience, but, it is the visual humour which reduces them to guffaws and belly-laughs. Everywhere, there is incongruity. This incongruity is supported by the large amount of colourful movement implicit in the stage directions.

Here is a scene with considerable comic force, much of which, as we have noted, comes from the dialogue. But, the stage directions give us the key to the *visual* humour. If we read a play without attempting to be aware of its visual implications, then both our understanding and enjoyment are incomplete.

THE THEATRICAL ELEMENTS

When you read a play, what are the especially theatrical elements to keep in mind as possible contributors to the picture you are attempting to piece together?

You should look principally at the stage directions, movement, music, dramatic tension, audience involvement, colour, and use of dialect within the work.

THE STAGE DIRECTIONS

This is the easiest 'orchestrative' element for the reader to locate, since it is always given in the text in black and white. Before you write a drama essay, always look to find out whether the stage directions make a significant contribution to the play in general and to the theme you are analysing in particular. By way of example, let us stay with the Brecht extract. See if you can decide in what way the stage directions contribute to the effectiveness of the action.

Now that you have thought over the possible effects, yourself, let us look at some of the directions in detail, imagining that you are the producer.

fährt herum: speed of action required to convey sense of shock.

starrt ihn entgeistert an : no speech from Schwiegermutter, therefore the quality of the physical gesture is important. She has to *look* 'entgeistert', with her mouth dropping open.

er klettert hervor: clambering noise and awkwardness to be rendered. Could use mosquito-net to good effect. Jussup could get caught in it for a moment or two.

steigt er aus: could make the climbing really awkward, or shaky.

schwankend, im Hemd: make the most of the tottering. Remember, he is a peasant. A long shirt; could be full of holes.

zitternd: let the audience be in no doubt that she is quivering.

erblicken ihn: astonishment, as they catch sight of Jussup.

schreien auf: force of *auf*. Let those screams rip!

noch auf den Knieen: contrast of Grusche in a Madonna-position. Could use spots.

dreht den Kopf herum: spots could highlight this movement.

MOVEMENT OR PACE

In order to keep the audience involved in the play, a good playwright will vary the movement or the pace of the action. When you are studying a play, always look to see what pace it has. There are several devices used to give a feeling of movement.

The first of these is the use of short scenes to balance the effect of longer ones. In the last act of *Maria Stuart*, for example, Schiller uses a relatively large number of shorter scenes to increase tension and to convey to the audience a feeling of a flood tide in the affairs of state, over which the humans involved appear to have no control, now that Elisabeth I is intent upon the destruction of her cousin, Maria. In these shorter scenes, there are many very brief speeches, which produce a staccato effect and help to counteract the longer utterances:

ELISABETH: Du kommst allein zurück – Wo sind die Lords?
PAGE: Mylord von Leicester und der Großschatzmeister –
ELISABETH: (*in der höchsten Spannung*) Wo sind sie?
PAGE: Sie sind nicht in London.
ELISABETH: Nicht? – Wo sind sie denn?
PAGE: Das wußte niemand mir zu sagen.
  Vor Tages Anbruch hätten beide Lords
  Eilfertig und geheimnisvoll die Stadt
  Verlassen.

The use of exchanges involving a number of short statements is also an important device open to the writer in plays with few scene changes, to instil a feeling of pace and movement. The prevailing atmosphere in Georg Kaiser's *Die Bürger von Calais* is inevitably one of claustrophobia, since the good citizens are incarcerated as hostages for almost the length of the play. However, even a deliberately constructed claustrophobia may need to be broken to give the audience relief and with it, a feeling of some sort of movement. Once again, this may be done by the infusion of passages of short, sharp dialogue:

EUSTACHE DE SAINT-PIERRE (*Rasch*): Hast du dein Los gegriffen?
PIERRE DE WISSANT: Eine ist übrig – ihr haltet sechs blaue Kugeln!

EUSTACHE DE SAINT-PIERRE (*schüttelt den Kopf*): Die Schüssel ist nicht leer – soll danach einer der Krüppel sie ausschütten?
(*Er schiebt die Schüssel näher zu ihm, der Dritte Bürger rückt sie schräg über den Tisch ganz dicht vor ihn.*)
PIERRE DE WISSANT (*zuckt die Ahseln, zieht das Tuch weg – stutzt und hebt langsam eine blaue Kugel heraus – stammelnd.*) Die letzte Kugel ist blau!
Um den Tisch ist es still.
JACQUES DE WISSANT (*nun die Seine hinstreckend*): Blau ist diese!
DER DRITTE BÜRGER (*ebenso*): Diese ist – wie die letzte!

The good citizens are drawing coloured balls to decide which one of them shall be sacrificed. The tension of a situation in which there has clearly been some tampering is accentuated by the brusque nature of the speech.

We will stay with Kaiser's expressionist masterpiece for a moment to consider another device employed to provide variety and to keep the audience enthralled. Often, as a relief from the spoken word, the playwright will introduce an extended series of stage-directions, through which speech is suppressed for a while and the audience has to concentrate on the evidence of its eyes, only. This device is particularly good for conveying tension and a certain immediacy, since it has something of the quality of mime. When no one speaks and you hear the silence, your concentration is very sharp, indeed:

Er [Jean de Vienne] geht nach rechts, ihm folgen einige – auch einer der ein Bündel trägt. Von links dringt klappernder Hall eines gemächlichen gleichmäßigen Schreitens, zugleich läuft von der Tiefe dort ein Flüstern. Auf der rechten Seite zeigen noch zögernd – dann rasch Arme hinüber – nun schwillt der zischelnde Lärm stärker auf : Der Erste!
DER FÜNFTE BÜRGER *kommt von links – er endigt seinen rüstigen Gang in der Marktmitte. Eine kleine Weile verharrt er steif – dann dreht er den Kopf weit nach rechts – nach links.*
   Es ist lautlos still geworden.
DER FÜNFTE BÜRGER *blickt vor sich auf den Boden – und tritt aus seinen Schuben. Danach richtet er das Gesicht nach oben – und beginnt mit festen Händen sein Kleid am Halse zu öffnen. Schultern und Arme sind entblößt – nun hält er es nur auf der Brust zusammen und wartet.*
EIN GEWÄHLTER BÜRGER *tritt von den anderen, rollt das Bündel auf und entnimmt einen wenig langen Strick – er stellt sich dicht hinter den fünften Bürger, hebt das sackförmige farblose Gewand hoch über ihn, streift es an ihm nieder: es hüllt ihn mit schwerem Hang ein, verschließt Arme und schleppt um die Füße. Nun weitet er die Schlinge – und legt sie auf die Schultern – das lose Seil im Rücken lassend.*

Attention could hardly be more strongly focussed than in these moments of preparation for an execution and, yet, after the anonymous 'Der erste!', not a word is spoken.

MUSIC

It is particularly easy to ignore the musical stage directions when reading a play. This is because it is hard to imagine the music, when in your class reading and in your essay preparation, you are concentrating on the thought and the words of which the play is built up. Yet, a little imagination can help you to realize how much the music may add to the scene and to the play as a whole.

For instance in the stage directions for Scene 1 of *Der kaukasische Kreidekreis* we read:

> Von der jungen Traktoristin geführt, tritt der Sänger Arkadi Tscheidse, ein stämmiger Mann von einfachem Wesen, in den Kreis. Mit ihm sind Musiker mit ihren Instrumenten. Die Künstler werden mit Händeklatschen begrüßt.

At intervals throughout the play, there are songs from the singer. The musicians, often a 3–5 piece jazz group, will be heard intermittently throughout the play. Brecht had originally introduced the singing and the music to reinforce his controversial *Verfremdungseffekt*, to remind us, the audience, that this is only a play and, in short, a play within a play. What actually also happens is that the singer, functioning somewhat like the chorus in classical Greek drama, provides another level of interest and the music of the band is welcomed for its colour and entertainment value.

Look for any use of music in the play you are studying and ask yourself: *how does the music enhance the total effect of the work?*

COLOUR

Unfortunately, when you read a play you are in a worse position than someone with a black and white television set who yearns for colour. At least this person has the advantage of being able to see the characters and the scene, to watch the movement and to hear the words, sound effects and music as they are actually produced.

You, with only the printed text in front of you, will often have no more than the stage directions to guide you. So, again, try to let your imagination take over. Find out what you can from the text as to what costumes are being worn, how rich the sets are, how much furniture and bric-a-brac is to be used. In a strange sort of way, this will help you to peg down the sometimes disembodied voices which come to you from the lines on the page.

Often the use of colour, or the partial suppression of it, may be crucial to the playwright's purpose. It is important, for instance, to know why in *Der kaukasische Kreidekreis* Brecht introduces highly colourful, flamboyant costumes and props for the members of the royal court, while he stipulates drab peasant-wear for so many of the other characters. Similarly, Büchner's insistence on total simplicity of dress with modest backcloths and few props in *Woyzeck* is of considerable significance. Always ask the question: *What use does the author make of colour in the play?*

DRAMATIC TENSION

This is an element which will require less delving on your part. If the play is read effectively in class, much of the tension will come out. Nonetheless, you will be even more aware of its presence, if you make a specific search for the devices which produce it. Look for:

1 clashes of personality or character
2 the mixing of long and short scenes
3 scenes containing a preponderance of short lines or speeches
4 a plot with many twists and turns
5 a *deus ex machina* (= a surprise intervention)
6 scenes ending on a high point
7 the frequent introduction of innuendo
8 misfortune befalling a sympathetic character
9 a race against time
10 protagonists acting in ignorance of a situation of which the audience have prior knowledge
11 strong emotional appeals to the audience
12 the introduction of characters symbolizing good and evil
13 gripping physical action
14 audience involvement

Many of the observations you make in relation to the dramatic tension of a play will also be relevant in essays on character, style, the author's position, the general worth of the work.

AUDIENCE INVOLVEMENT

This is a feature of many plays of which you may not be aware, unless you have been to the theatre quite often. Again, the stage direction may be of help to you, but, often, a producer will take the decision for him or herself to involve patrons in certain parts of the play.

This may be nothing more than the colourful pantomime technique of having everybody join in a song with some of the characters. On the other hand, a character being chased may run into the audience, passing through the rows and along the steps, as (s) he goes.

Alternatively, one of the principals may address specific individuals in the audience from the boards and may even go as far as expecting an answer from them. He or she may occasionally leave the boards and talk with the people in the auditorium. (S)he may ridicule them or appeal to their sense of reason.

When you are reading a play in class, look for the possibilities for such audience involvement.

DIALECT

When reading the text of the play, it is easy to ignore the most obvious speech-related device which the author will use. Somehow, we have long fallen into the trap of believing that *proper* plays are spoken in *proper* accents, otherwise known as *received pronunciation* or *standard English*.

This process of *standardization* used to be common to both the English and

German theatres, but the last twenty years have seen a movement back towards the use of normal, natural accents in plays, as the playwrights intended them to sound.

In *Der Hauptmann von Köpenick*, Carl Zuckmayer makes it difficult for those who would have ordinary people talk with drawing-room accents. Voigt, the main character and an old lag, speaks a very distinctive Berlin dialect.

Ick weiß nich, Herr Kommissär, ick werde in letzter Zeit immer leichter. Besonders seit ick aus der Plötze raus bin, da hab' ick fast nur noch Luft in den Knochen.

Heinrich von Kleist's comedy, *Der zerbrochene Krug*, was written in another age and this is reflected in the way the peasant characters speak Hochdeutsch. Listen, for example, to Frau Marthe:

Nichts seht ihr, Verlaub, die Scherben seht ihr;
Der Kruge schönster ist entzweigeschlagen.
Hier grade auf dem Loch, wo jetzo nichts,
Sind die gesamten niederländischen Provinzen
Dem spanschen Philipp übergeben worden.

This is very different from Voigt's way of talking. Yet, the two should be closer together. A level of reality can be introduced here, by allowing Frau Marthe to speak with a regional accent and intonation. If you are reading a German play in your group and you have an Assistent (in), ask him or her to help you acquire a regional accent for any character whose social standing does not prohibit it. Remember that local accents bring vigour to speech in a way in which received pronunciation rarely can. Remember also that, like most of us, a character does not have to be a 'rough diamond' to speak with a regional accent. Look at the characters in the play under study, imagine them with local accents or not, as appropriate, and decide how much you feel the action of the play to be enhanced.

ASSIGNMENTS

1 Select 6 stage directions from a play you have been studying and show how they are intended to affect the audience's involvement and reactions.
2 Give 6 instances from the text of a play to show the level of movement or the lack of it.
3 If music is used to any extent in your play, give examples from the text to show its function.
4 Give 6 examples of the ways in which your playwright maintains the dramatic tension.
5 Show how you think a local dialect might be introduced to good effect into the production of your play.
6 What are the possibilities for audience involvement in your play? Give 6 instances from the text of points in the action where the audience might be brought in.

9

The poetry essay

The poetry essay differs radically in certain respects from the other types discussed, since it demands even closer attention to techniques than to themes. It is not so much a question of *what* the poet achieves as *how* (s)he does so. The finished effect will be achieved by use, skilful or otherwise, of metre, intonation, rhyme, alliteration assonance, original imagery, musicality and other devices.

Because also of the peculiar ability of poetry to achieve an emotional response in the listener-reader, the poet will often be trying to reach us via our feelings. However high our own intellectualism, the fundamental appeal of most poetry is to the senses, and we respond to the powerful combination of sounds and pictures offered in any good poem. Therefore we will frequently be looking for the effect of a particular choice of a word, or of a combination of words, or of a stylistic device.

Let us concentrate on the implications of the poet's technique, since the material practised in many of the other chapters in this book will help you with the other aspects of the poetry essay. First, we need to look at the types of question set by the examining Boards. These may be divided roughly into two groups:

Group A
1 Do you find anything in the work of . . . which is relevant to the modern reader?
2 Which poem or group of poems by . . . has made the greatest impression on you?
3 Compare and contrast the views of society expressed in the following poems by . . . and . . .
4 In what sense is . . .'s poetry a reaction against the times?
5 Discuss . . .'s treatment of the theme of . . . in his poetry.
6 Trace the main developments in German poetry since Novalis.

Group B
1 From the poetry in your selection, choose any two poems on the same theme and discuss the writer's treatment of it.
2 Based on your reading of the poems in the collection, what evidence is there for considering . . . , . . . , and . . . to belong to a recognizable poetic movement?
3 How far is poem A or poem B characteristic of its author?

4 Where, in your opinion, do . . . 's strengths and weaknesses as a poet lie?
5 Discuss the characteristic features of . . .'s response to death/nature/night/ society. Make detailed reference to at least four poems.
6 Whis poet in the collection has had the greatest appeal for you and for what reasons?

In Group A we are concerned principally with themes, and points of style, though important, are likely to take second place.

In Group B, however, the emphasis will be at least as much on questions of style, method and technique, as on themes. Thus, essays on this type of question should contain much more of a balance between the analysis of ideas and the means of conveying them.

If the topic on which you have to write falls into category B, then you may find it easier to organize your material into two separate sections, one dealing with thematic points, the other with stylistic items. You may also find it easier to deal with themes and general implications first and to analyse the poet's style in the latter stages of your essay, much after the manner of the strong treatment referred to in Chapter 3.

POETIC DEVICES

In order to analyse a poet's style and to make valid comments upon it, you need to be able to identify the various concrete elements from which a poem is built-up. Once you can do this, it is not too difficult to pinpoint the particular quality of a poet's work with a fair degree of accuracy.

Study the list of devices below and look for examples of them in the poems you have been studying during your course.

EXTERNAL PATTERNS

Metre

The *metre* is the type of rhythm which has been used to write the poem. Before we continue to discuss the various aspects of metre in German poetry, it is worth pausing a moment to look at the way English, German and French are spoken.

Find someone who speaks good French (possibly yourself) and ask her or him to speak the following three sentences with a sheet of thin paper held six inches (fifteen centimetres) or so in front of the mouth:

My cousin is representing Great Britain at the Olympiad.
Meine Kusine repräsentiert Großbritannien bei der Olympiade.
Ma cousine représente la Grande Bretagne à l'Olympiade.

What did you notice? If the experiment was carried out without any accidental or deliberate interference by the speaker, the sheet of paper should have moved much more as the English and German words were spoken than for the French. Like Ivor the Engine, we use a lot of puff when we speak either of the sister, Anglo-Germanic languages.

Now, let us take the question of our breath and the way it comes out a little further. It will help you to understand the breath-speech mechanism if you think of English/German on the one hand and French on the other as two instruments in the jazz orchestra. The Germanic languages sound like a drum and *beat* out the rhythm. French is much more like the characteristic sound of the trombone, where notes *glide* out and syncopation occurs, i.e. the trombone notes glide across the beat. We can look at it diagrammatically.

The English/German drum: ′ ′ ′ ′ ′ ′ ′ ′ ′ ′
The French trombone: ⌣ ⌣ ⌣ ⌣ ⌣ ⌣ ⌣

Put them together in the orchestra and you have:

So, the hallmark of the way native English and German speakers speak is the beat. As poetry is a *spoken* art form, the main, underlying characteristic of an English or German poem will be its beat, its rhythm, its metre.

There are four basic rhythms which provide metre in the poetry of our two languages. These are the *iam*, the *trochee*, the *anapaest* and the *dactyl*. Of these, by far the most common, because it reflects the basic pattern of speech, is the *iambic* rhythm, a two-syllable foot, the first unstressed, the second stressed

In tiefĕr Naćht, wĕnn aúf dem schmalĕn Stegĕ
          Dĕr Wańdrĕr bebt.   Goethe: *Nähe des Geliebten*

This example was chosen to make an important point right at the beginning of this section on poetic devices. You may well have noticed that (a) the second line was much shorter than the first and (b) there was an extra syllable at the end of the first line, after the five iams.

There is a certain freedom in the German line, which dates from the latter part of the eighteenth century, when Goethe and others during their *Sturm und Drang* period fought hard and successfully to free German verse from unnecessary constraints. So, do not expect everything in the line and stanza to be always completely regular.

The *trochee* is another two-syllable foot and is the reverse of the iam, i.e. the first syllable is stressed and the second unstressed (′ ˘):

Frühlĭng lässt sĕin blauĕs Bánd
Wiedĕr fláttĕrn duŕch dĭe Lüftĕ.   Mörike: *Er ist's*

Once again, what do you notice about the first line of the quotation?

The *anapaest* is a three-syllable foot, containing two unstressed syllables, followed by one stressed (˘ ˘ ′). Frequently, poems may contain a mixture of anapaests and other metres, as here:

És klírrtĕn dĭe Béchĕr, eš jaúchzteň dĭe Knećht',
Šo kláng eš dĕm stórrigĕn Kóniğĕ rećht.

Heine: *Belsazar*

Which is the other metre used here? Yes, it is the iam. Heine's specific purpose in using the mixture of iams and anapaests is to quicken the rhythm of the poem.

The *dactyl* is the other three-syllable foot and contains one stressed syllable, followed by two unstressed (´ ˘ ˘). Like the anapaest, it is often used in combination with another metric form:

Liebllch wár dĭe Máieňnaćht
Sílbĕrwölkleĭn flógĕn
Oɓ dĕr hóldĕn Frühlĭngsprăcht,
Freudĭg híngĕzógĕn.

Lenau: *Der Postillon*

Here, Lenau uses a basic trochaic rhythm, with the first and third lines ending in a dactyl.

The mixture can sometimes be more complex, as in:

Eš sćhienĕn sŏ góldĕn dĭe Sterňe
....
Sićh stúrzeň iň diĕ Wáldešnacht.

Eichendorff: *Sehnsucht*

In the first of these lines, we have an iam, followed by two anapaests and a final unstressed syllable. In the second line there are three consecutive unaccented syllables. Eichendorff uses these devices to help render the pleasant, idealised landscape of a moonlit summer's night.

INDIVIDUAL PATTERNS AND FREE VERSE

Broken rhythms

One characteristic of modern verse is the freeing of the poet from what had been referred to as the 'tyranny' of rhyme and metre. A large proportion of present-day poetry is written in totally free verse. When the mood took him, Goethe was writing with such freedom two hundred years ago. In *Prometheus*, for example, he uses broken rhythms to produce an emotive and aggressive conversational tone, to show his disgust with the Gods:

Ich kenne nichts Ärmeres
Unter der Sonn' als euch, Götter!
· Ihr nähret kümmerlich
Von Opfersteuern. . .

Irregular line length

Without striving for the particular effect which Goethe achieved above, a poet may vary the length of line for a variety of reasons. Here, Mörike introduces a deliberately shortened line, to anticipate and underline the importance of what follows and to slow the pace:

> Und kecker rauschen die Quellen hervor,
> Sie singen der Mutter, der Nacht, ins Ohr
>   Vom Tage,
> Vom heute gewesenen Tage.
>
> *Um Mitternacht*

Alternation of longer and shorter lines

This is a technique which, once again, may be introduced to produce a variety of effects. Generally speaking, the shortness of a line makes us focus attention on it. In the example below, the short lines accentuate the dramatic character of the narrative. In lines 2 and 4, we can hear the tread of the stately lion and the concept of *bedächtig* is conveyed in the heavy syllables of the last line:

> Und hinein mit bedächtigem Schritt
>   Ein Löwe tritt
> Und sieht sich stumm
>   Rings um.
>
> Schiller: *Der Handschuh*

INTERNAL DEVICES

Assonance

Assonance is a form of internal rhyme, in which the poet uses a concentration of the same or similar vowel sounds. In the example, Mörike employs a cluster of *umlaut*-ed vowels, to convey the peaceful insistence of the night after the lively day:

> Hört man der Erdenkräfte flüsterndes Gedränge,
> Das aufwärts in die zärtlichen Gesänge
> Der reingestimmten Lüfte summt.
>
> *Gesang zu zweien in der Nacht*

Alliteration

Alliteration is the other form of internal rhyme. Here, the poet makes frequent use of the same or similar consonants. In the example, Schiller draws on several hard consonants (w, t, s, m in particular) to give the feel of raging waters. The sound achieved is quite cacophonous (see below):

> Und es wallet und siedet und brauset und zischt
> Wie wenn Wasser mit Feuer sich mengt.
>
> *Der Taucher*

Elision

Elision is the suppression or omission of a vowel or syllable, usually to help the line scan properly or to soften the effect of the word(s):

Sie achtet's nicht, sie ist es müd',
Ihr klingt des Himmels Bläue süßer noch
Der flücht' gen Stunden gleichgeschwung' nes Joch.

Mörike: *Um Mitternacht*

Cacophony

The literal meaning of cacophony is *discordant sound* and the device is used by the poet when (s)he wants to assault the listener's ear, by means of the harsh quality of the sound:

Und die *Fl*ammen *f*ressen brennend *W*ald um *W*ald,
Ge*l*be/*Fl*edermäuse,/*z*ac*k*ig/in/das/*L*aub/ge*k*ra*llt*,
Seine/Stange/haut/er/wie/ein/*K*öhler*k*necht/
In/die/*B*äume,/daß/das Feuer/*b*rause/recht.

Heym: *Der Krieg*

Where there is alliteration, it is of harsh consonants. Heym deliberately chooses hard-sounding words, which do not run smoothly into each other. There is an abruptness and one can hear the cruelty of the flames. The sound is enough to tell us how War has re-awakened disorder and has brought its usual destruction with it.

Onomatopoeia

A word or phrase is said to be onomatopoeic if its sound conveys an idea of its actual sense or meaning, e.g. *stottern* – to stutter. In poetry, this may be extended, so that the lines give an idea of the action through their rhythms and the way they sound. In the following extract, Goethe produces a metrical arrangement which suggests the regular beat of horses' hooves:

Dem Schnee, dem Regen,
Dem Wind entgegen,
Im Dampf der Klüfte,
Durch Nebeldüfte,
Immer zu! Immer zu!
Ohne Rast und Ruh'.

Rastlose Liebe

Here, Goethe is at pains to create an impression of restlessness and to achieve this, he produces a series of short, even abrupt phrases without a subject or verb.

End-stopping

This term simply means the occurrence of a punctuation mark at the end of a line. Such marks are nothing more than a written means of indicating breath-pauses.

Thus, when a stanza is heavily end-stopped, the pace of the poem is slowed down:

Der Kümmernisberg steht gläsern still,
Vor alle Ziele gestellt.
Und wer in süßere Meilen nun will,
Dem steht er vor der welt.

Loerke: Sommernachts über Land

Enjambement

Enjambement occurs when a sense grouping of words runs beyond the end of one line into the first words of the next. It can be used to create many different effects such as a rushing flow of thoughts or events or, as in the example below, to bring the reader's attention to the important points of the philosophical argument:

Ich gestehe es: ich
Habe keine Hoffnung.
Die Blinden reden von einem Ausweg. Ich
Sehe.

Brecht: Der Nachgeborene

Note how, because of the run-on effect of enjambement, the reader's attention is drawn to the second and fourth lines. The word(s) necessary to complete the sense of the preceding line (in our example 'habe keine Hoffnung' and 'Sehe') is/are known as the *rejet*.

Enumeration (listing)

This device is used principally for climax/emphasis and/or to stimulate the listener's emotions/imagination:

Sie singen von Lenz und Liebe, von sel'ger goldner Zeit,
Von Freiheit, Männerwürde, von Treu' und Heiligkeit.

Uhland: Des Sängers Fluch

Here, it is used for dramatic effect and to evoke something of a surge of nostalgia.

Stimmungsbrechung

The *Stimmungsbrechung* signifies an abrupt change of mood, through which the listener/reader, having suspended his/her disbelief, and entered into the feel and spirit of the poem, is brought back sharply to the realities of life. This device is characteristic of the (Romantic) ballad and is also used in a somewhat up-dated manner by Heinrich Heine, who seems to delight in creating a mood into which he can draw his readers, only to bring them back abruptly to consciousness at his own whim.

Out in a boat on the North Sea, the poet catches a glimpse of the ghost of a young girl at a window. He is about to fall into the water –

Aber zur rechten Zeit noch
Ergriff mich beim Fuß der Kapitän,
Und zog mich vom Schiffsrand,
Und rief, ärgerlich lachend:
Doktor, sind Sie des Teufels?.

Heine: Seegespenst

Personification
This is a frequent device (used especially by the Romantics) in which natural
phenomena, objects and animals are given human form, or their actions are
described as if they were those of human beings:

Wenn Weste seinen Spiegel küssen
Des Ufers Blume fühlt es nicht.

Droste-Hühlshoff: Der Weiher

NINETEENTH AND TWENTIETH CENTURY GERMAN POETRY

The section which follows outlines some of the major features you are likely to
find in the Romantic poetry of the nineteenth century. Some themes – such as the
death-wish for example – have survived into the poetry of this century, and in so
doing, illustrate the dangers of over-categorizing themes, individual poems, or
poets into a particular school or movement. The features listed below should be
considered together, since they all contribute to the Romantic world-view,
powered as it was by the desire to escape from an increasingly industrial and
materialistic society.

German poetry of the twentieth century has also been influenced in form and
content by the social, political and economic upheavals that have taken place.
Reactions to these influences have been varied, but as we shall see later, some
notable characteristics in form alone can be identified.

CHARACTERISTICS OF THE ROMANTIC MOVEMENT

The poetry is likely to be highly subjective.
It may include a preference for a world of fantasy or of the exotic.
It will be highly individualistic.
There may be an expressed or implicit desire to commune with Nature. This
may often be as a result of dissatisfaction with the environment.
There may therefore be a tendency to seek escape in other ages and climes.
There is often a glorification of the German Middle Ages.
Dissatisfaction may develop into a morbid yearning for the unobtainable, the
extreme form of which will be the poet's Weltschmerz (see below).
There will frequently be a personification of natural and inanimate objects,
with the establishment of an intimate relationship between the poet and such
objects. These objects may be treated as sentient beings.

For the Romantic poet, the sensation of the moment is supreme. Consequently, some Romantic poetry may verge on the incoherent. Many Romantic poets were exceptionally fond of music. This may be conveyed to the reader by the musicality of the verse.

The death-wish

Characteristic of German Romantic poetry is the death-wish (der Wille zum Tode), in which the poet or the characters (s)he has created express a world-weariness and a desire to depart this life. The death-wish continues to occupy a significant place in the literature of the twentieth century and has been closely analysed and explained by Sigmund Freud, the father of modern psychology. Here is an example of the death-wish in its most straightforward expression:

> Und weiter reitet der Reitersmann,
> Und seufzet schwer dazu:
> So zieh ich denn hin ins Grab so früh, –
> Wohlan, im Grab ist Ruh!

Heine: *Bergstimme*

Weltschmerz

The Weltschmerz is another phenomenon which is characteristic of Romantic poetry and is closely related to the death-wish. It is more a form of world-weariness and for the Romantics, escape from the pain of the world is usually afforded by Night, their friend and comforter:

> Nimm mit deinem Zauberdunkel
> Diese Welt von hinnen mir.

Lenau: *Bitte*

The Volkslied

From the time of Herder and the young Goethe onwards, the Volkslied greatly influenced German poetry, as far as the end of the nineteenth century. Unless you are studying the modernists of our own century, much of the lyric poetry you are likely to encounter will have been influenced at least in part by the Volkslied and its most common form, the ballad.

Volkslied characteristics include:

A lament by the disappointed lover.

A ballad-type refrain.

The deliberate use of archaisms.

The association of the loved one with an inanimate object or with the natural elements.

The inclusion of supernatural elements.

The expression of the abstract in terms of concrete images, e.g. a ring may symbolise fidelity.

A restless yearning.

A need for escape/a Wanderlust.

An abrupt ending in which the mood is deliberately broken.
An obsession with or a reversion to the Middle Ages.

TWENTIETH CENTURY INNOVATIONS

The upheavals of our century have had an inevitable influence on the way poetry
has developed. The most obvious innovation has been the *apparent* formlessness
of some of the poetry produced. Two ways in which this may be achieved are
illustrated below.

The omission of verbs
In this example of highly ejaculatory poetry, Gottfried Benn suppresses any hint
of a verb, to create nihilistic, isolated verse, which is typical of the Expressionist
period:

> Ein Wort-, ein Glanz, ein Flug, ein Feuer,
> ein Flammenwurf, ein Sternenstrich-,
> und wieder Dunkel, ungeheuer,
> im leeren Raum um Welt und Ich.

Ein Wort, ein Satz

The suppression of syntax
In this next example, Benn goes further and omits all other impressions of syntax,
as well as the verbs:

> VERLORENES Ich, zersprengt von Stratosphären,
> Opfer des Ion –: Gamma-Strahlen-Lamm –,
> Teilchen und Feld –: Unendlichkeitschimären
> auf deinem grauen Stein von Notre Dame.

Verlorenes Ich

These lines convey very clearly indeed Gottfried Benn's disillusionment with a
world of chaos in which Art is the only stability.

ASSIGNMENTS

1 Match each critical comment with the correct quotation.

i	da wird' still, Und herum im Kreis, Von Mordsucht heiβ, Lagern die greulichen Katzen.

ii | Der Bestienblick: die Sterne als Kaldaunen,
der Dschungeltod als Seins- und Schöpfungsgrund,
Mensch, Volkerschlachten, Katalaunen,
hinab den Bestienschlund.

iii | Am Nachmittag stellt sie mir eine Tasse Kaffee
Neben meine Schreibmaschine,
Schwarz mit einem Löffel Zucker, und ich trinke,
Und sie fragt mich, was ich schreib'.

iv | Bedecke deinen Himmel, Zeus,
Mit Wolkendunst
Und übe, dem Knaben gleich,
Der Disteln köpft,
An Eichen dich und Bergeshöhn;

v | Sie hat mir Treu' versprochen,
Gab mir ein'n Ring dabei,
Sie hat die Treu' gebrochen,
Mein Ringlein sprang entzwei.

vi | Mein Vater, mein Vater, und hörest du nicht,
Was Erlenkönig mir leise verspricht?

vii | Weil' auf mir, du dunkles Auge,
Übe deine ganze Macht,
Ernste, milde, träumerische,
Unergründlich süße Nacht!

viii | Mit diesem I-A, I-A, dem Geweih'r,
Dem schluchzend ekelhaften Mißlaut, brachte
Mich zur Verzweiflung schier das dumme Tier,
Ich selbst zuletzt schrie auf – und ich erwachte.

ix | An dem Himmel herauf mit leisen Schritten
Kommt die duftende Nacht; ihr folgt die süße
Liebe. Ruhet und liebet!

x | Die zerflackenden Bäume mit Trauer zu schwärzen,
Brauste ein Sturm. Sie verbrannten wie Blut,
Untergehend, schon fern.

(a) Here, Schiller uses enjambement to convey a sense of urgency and anticipation.

(b) The large number of stressed syllables produces lines which ring with the unmistakable sound of horses hooves.

(c) The lack of an obvious sentence-structure in these lines, reflects the author's rebellion against an over-structured society which has produced its own form of chaos.

(d) Here, Lenau employs apostrophe and accumulation to convey a mixture of reverence and ecstasy.

(e) The *Stimmungsbrechung* in the final lines of this quotation is typical of Heine's tendency towards an abrupt change of mood and of his delight in manipulating those for whom he writes.

(f) Note how the heavily end-stopped lines give weight and solemnity to the verse, reflecting the picture the poet is painting.

(g) The poet's use of blank verse allows the line to flow naturally, since we do not anticipate the rhyme. This gentle flow is well-suited to the recounting of ordinary domestic activities and emphasises the quiet intimacy existing between poet and beloved.

(h) Goethe uses apostrophe here for altogether different reasons, to produce a form of almost button-holing familiarity, which underlines Prometheus's contempt for the mighty beings whom he is addressing.

(i) The obvious symbolism, straightforward vocabulary and partially repeated refrain are typical of the *Volkslied*.

(j) The poet uses predominantly hard consonants to produce something near to cacophony. The words seem isolated one from another and convey an impression of primaeval natural forces, intent on destruction.

2 For each passage, choose the correct completion for the critical comment:

> 1 | Horch! das Feuerglöcklein gellt:
> Hinterm Berg,
> Hinterm Berg
> Brennt es in der Mühle!

(Mörike: Der Feuerreiter)

In the two shorter lines, Mörike uses . . . . to imitate the rhythm of the horse.

a) iams
b) dactyls
c) trochees
d) spondees.

> 2 | O Herr, ich falle auf das Knie:
> Sei gnädig meiner letzten Stund!
> Das Jahr ist um!

(Droste-Hülshoff: Am Letzten Tage des Jahres)

The last line of the poem is, like the first one, deliberately short to convey an impression of . . .

a) joy
b) resentment
c) anticipation
d) finality.

> 3 | Wir bauen an dir mit zitternden Händen
> und wir türmen Atom auf Atom.
> Aber wer kann dich vollenden,
> du Dom?

(Rilke: Wir bauen an dir)

The personification of *du Dom* and the prominence it is given in a short line of its own emphasise Rilke's sense of . . .

a) wonderment and piety.
b) isolation
c) Weltschmerz
d) humour.

> 4 | Zuweilen geht ein Wimmern, wie verloren,
> Dann stirbt im toten Wald ein Reh.

(Liliencron: *Heide im Winter*)

The soft w's and t's convey another level of . . . to the scene.

 a) violence
 b) desolation
 c) celebration
 d) aggression.

> 5 | dann hat die Seele Ruh';
> Tastend streift sie ab die Wanderschuh.

(Keller: *Abendlied*)

The image of the Soul slipping off its walking boots is excessively. . .

 a) trite
 b) lyrical
 c) pathetic
 d) modern

> 6 | Wie messe ich, ohne zu messen, den Flug der Tauben,
> So hoch und tief er blitzt, so tief und hoch mir ein!

(Loerke: *Strom*)

The inverted repetition in this last line . . . the surging flight of the pigeons.

 a) contrasts with
 b) parodies
 c) mimics
 d) criticises.

3 Make notes on the verse forms of the poems in your collection.
4 Use the check-list and analyse the types of rhyme used by your poet(s).
5 Take any one or two poems by *one* poet and, using the check-list to help you, make notes on the vocabulary used.
6 Work through your collection of poems and find examples of as many different figures of speech as possible.
7 Using examples a–i as a guide, select an important 1–5 line quote from each of your poems and write a short paragraph of commentary on it.
8 Isolate and make notes on the separate themes which occupy your poet(s).

9 Compare and contrast the treatment of a similar theme in two different poems.
10 Take any one of the topics in Group A on page 64, fill in the gap(s) to suit your author and draw up a rough draft for an essay.
11 Do the same with any Group B topic on pages 64–5.

10

The context question

Many students try to avoid context questions, because they are afraid of them and tend to see them as a trap. They think that the question has been set simply as a difficult memory test, requiring a very exact identification of a passage and not much more.

It will help you to feel easier about this type of literary assignment, if you can accept that it has a more creative purpose than simply to force students into working at a book, head down, trying to memorize the layout of the work.

WHAT IS THE CONTEXT QUESTION?

It is not a translation exercise or an opportunity to tell the story. Part of its intention, admittedly, is to discover whether you have read the work thoroughly, but it also attempts to find out whether you have read it with understanding and whether you have the ability to analyse a small and often highly significant piece of text.

Therefore, if you have made a mistake in identifying a passage, take heart! You may still be able to do quite well with the question as a whole, if your general understanding and analysis of the passage are of a good standard.

HOW SHOULD ONE SET ABOUT TACKLING A CONTEXT QUESTION?

It is just as well to ask this, since Examination Boards often give you little guidance as to how to structure your answer. Others, however, are helpfully specific.

Generally speaking, you will not go far wrong if you divide your answer into the following four sections:

1 Identifying the location of the passage
2 A commentary on the passage
3 The significance of the passage
4 Points of special interest

1 LOCATING THE PASSAGE

Since the title of the assignment is the *context* question, it is possible to develop a fixation about this section of your answer and to go to *great lengths* to complete it. However, it is not necessary to write at great length about where the passage (or whole poem) occurs in the work.

On the contrary, your answer is likely to be all the better for an economical statement of where the extract occurs.

2   A COMMENTARY ON THE PASSAGE

This is a trap for the unwary. It is not an exercise in translation or paraphrasing. You are required to work through the passage analysing the meaning of the lines in relation to the work as a whole. Pages 84 and 86 give a clear example of this procedure. Note how it avoids giving a word-for-word translation of every line, but picks up, instead, their significance.

3   THE SIGNIFICANCE OF THE PASSAGE

Here, you comment on the relevance of the extract to the work as a whole. Start by asking yourself *Why was this passage chosen?* Does it:

(a) encapsulate main themes?
(b) reflect the author's aims and concerns?
(c) occur at a vital stage?
(d) affect the reader (audience) strongly?
(e) present the author at his (her) best/worst?
(f) present a typical example of the author's style?

4   POINTS OF SPECIAL INTEREST

These may relate to:

(a) the author's style
(b) (auto)biographical detail
(c) historical detail
(d) parallel work by other authors
(e) topical reference

THE POETRY CONTEXT QUESTION

This has somewhat different requirements from the other two *genres*, since, with poetry, you have to look for a large number of specific points. Below is a checklist of the points.

POETRY CONTEXT CHECKLIST

Section A Placing the passage in its context

1 Give the name of the poem, the poet and the collection from which it comes (e.g. 'Lyrisches Intermezzo', *Neue Gedichte*–Erster Teil).
2 State at which point in the poem the extract occurs.

3 Say how it fits into the general structure.
4 State very briefly (in one sentence) if it is typical of the poet's attitude (to poetry, nature, love, religion, society, his/her own life) and whether it can be related to his or her background or experience.

Section B The theme of the passage

5 State briefly in your own words the theme of the passage.
6 Do not paraphrase.
7 Give the basic idea, pointing out the key line(s) or stanza.
8 Show how this basic idea or emotion is amplified and illustrated by the rest of the extract.
9 Comment very briefly on the clarity or otherwise of the statement of the idea.

Section C Comment on the style of the passage

10 Comment on the figures of speech used.
11 Comment on the nature of the vocabulary, especially on the choice of verbs, adjectives and adverbs.
12 State whether the vocabulary is simple or elaborate, concrete or abstract, emotive or sensuous. Is there a good choice of individual words, giving a clear, vivid picture? Is there any use of colourful, evocative proper names? Are words chosen for their sound as well as for their meaning?
Are the similes and metaphors original and striking? Are they illuminating? Do they contain a wealth of meaning and of associations? Are they far-fetched? Ridiculous? Trite?
Is personification used. If so, does it present ideas more vividly?
How much repetition is there? Is it used for dramatic or musical effect? Is there any use made of other devices such as climax, enumeration, apostrophe?
13 What is the effect of the rhythm? Is there a musical quality? Describe the rhythm briefly. Is it smooth or broken, slow or rapid, etc.? What use is made of open or closed vowels?
14 Refer to the verse-form used by the poet. Comment on the type of stanza, the length of line, the rhythm, enjambement, variation in line-length, lines with an odd number of syllables. Is the poem a sonnet and is it regular or irregular?
15 Refer to the rhyme and its type.
16 How much use has been made of assonance and alliteration. In short, how far does the sound of the poem correspond to its sense?
There is a considerable amount of material to be covered here and when you have a very finite amount of time at your disposal to answer an exam question (usually an hour at most), it is unlikely you will be able to deal with every item in the above list. Therefore, you will have to judge for yourself your priorities (as has occurred in the sample answer on page 82). Some material may have to be left out and your own order of listing will vary from the above.

ASSIGNMENT

Read the sample context answers which follow, note the strategies used, consult
with your teacher, choose suitable passages in your own set books and attempt
your answers, following the headings given in the samples.

> Wir sprachen von Sturm und Schiffbruch,
> Vom Seemann, und wie er lebt,
> Und zwischen Himmel und Wasser
> Und Angst und Freude schwebt.
>
> Wir sprachen von fernen Küsten,
> Vom Süden und vom Nord,
> Und von den seltsamen Völkern
> Und seltsamen Sitten dort.
>
> Am Ganges duftet's und leuchtet's,
> Und Riesenbäume blühn,
> Und schöne, stille Menschen
> Vor Lotosblumen knien.
>
> In Lappland sind schmutzige Leute,
> Plattköpfig, breitmäulig und klein;
> Sie kauern ums Feuer, und backen
> Sich Fische, und quäken und schrein.
>
> Die Mädchen horchten ernsthaft,
> Und endlich sprach niemand mehr;
> Das Schiff war nicht mehr sichtbar,
> Es dunkelte gar zu sehr.

The location of the passage
The extract is the major part of Heinrich Heine's poem *Wir saßen am
Fischerhause*, from which the initial (two) stanzas have been omitted. The poem
belongs to the group of poems known as *Die Heimkehr* and it was written as a
consequence of a summer stay at Cuxhaven on the Baltic Coast.

The main theme
The poem is a synthesis of many of the principal themes in Heine's work and life,
communicating his love of both the North Sea and more exotic lands, his feelings
for the night, his love of both company and solitude and his abiding Weltschmerz.
Despite the references to far-off, colourful lands, it is Heine's awareness of the
duality of existence, of pain and joy, of beauty and ugliness which comes through
most strongly in the poem, particularly as he employs a dismissive
Stimmungsbrechung to bring himself and his reader out of a mood of exotic
reverie. In fact, there is the distinct impression that after a wide-ranging
discussion brought about by the sight of a lone ship out at sea, Heine has lost
interest in his topic.

In a sense, the main theme of the poem is as much his own intransigence, as a consideration of the dangers of life at sea and of those people who inhabit distant coasts. Characteristic of Heine's intransigence is his loss of patience with himself for indulging his exoticism, when there is so much ugliness in the world to counterbalance the attractions of oriental lands.

The style of the passage
The verse-form is iambic with a rhyming-pattern *abcb*, *a* and *c* often being feminine. This form, couched in lines which are for the most part relatively short, is well-suited to conveying a mood of quiet contemplation, which will be broken by an aggressively stated contrast.

In the course of the poem, Heine uses alliteration to achieve a variety of effects. In stanza 2, he employs a soft 'w' and 'f' to create an impression of distance, isolation and quietude:

> Und in der weiten Ferne
> Ward noch ein Schiff entdeckt.

In stanza 4, he uses a long 'z' sound together with a soft 'v' to give an impression of timelessness and of far-off places:

> Vom Süden und vom Nord,
> Und von den seltsamen Völkern
> Und seltsamen Sitten dort.

To create an altogether different effect, he introduces cacophony, to jolt himself and his reader out of their indulgence:

> Plattköpfig, breitmäulig und klein;
> Sie kauern ums Feuer, und backen
> Sich Fische, und quäcken und schrein.

Here, he uses hard consonants to begin many of the words and to separate them. He even includes the hard '-k' internally, to produce sound which is as unpleasant as the picture he has in mind.

There is a strong oriental influence in *Wir saßen am Fischerhause* and Heine employs some familiar conceits – the lotus flower, which we have already encountered in *Auf Flügeln des Gesanges* and *Die Lotusblume ängstigt sich*, both from *Lyrisches Intermezzo*, and the Ganges (*Auf Flügeln des Gesanges*). It is also quite typical of Heine that a consideration of the exotic and the voluptuous Orient should have been triggered by thoughts relating to the hard realities of life at sea. This is a clear example of the polarity of thought which is often Heine's hallmark and is well rendered in the antitheses of lines 11 and 12:

> Und zwischen Himmel und Wasser
> Und Angst und Freude schwebt.

The contrasts drawn in these lines give a very clear impression of the fragility of the sailors' position, when the elements see to it that they are so frequently balanced between life and death. But, of course, Heine is not simply referring to the insecurity of the seamen's position. The statement is equally a reflection of his own Weltschmerz. Fundamentally, it is the pain and insecurity of his own life which provoke the frequent abrupt changes of mood, of which the violent Stimmungsbrechung in the penultimate stanza is an all too obvious symptom. One might say that it is pure Heine. It is certainly the strongest impression we retain of *Wir saßen am Fischerhause*, a long time after having read it.

> Und plötzlich, wie unter einer Erinnerung, einem Impuls, wandte er den Oberkörper, eine Hand in der Hüfte, in schöner Drehung aus seiner Grundpositur und blickte über die Schulter zum Ufer.
>
> Der Schauende dort saß, wie er einst gesessen, als zuerst, von jener Schwelle zurückgesandt, dieser dämmergraue Blick dem seinen begegnet war. Sein Haupt war an der Lehne des Stuhles langsam der Bewegung des draußen Schreitenden gerolet; nun hob es sich, gleichsam dem Blicke entgegen, und sank auf die Brust, so daß seine Augen von unten sahen, indes sein Antlitz den schlaffen, innig versunkenen Ausdruck tiefen Schlummers zeigte. Ihm war aber, als ob der bleiche und liebliche Psychagog dort draußen ihm lächle; ihm winke; als ob er, die Hand aus der Hüfte lösend, hinausdeute, voranschwebe ins Verheißungsvoll-Ungeheure. Und wie so oft, machte er sich auf, ihm zu folgen.
>
> Minuten vergingen, bis man dem seitlich im Stuhle Hinabgesunkenen zu Hilfe eilte. Man brachte ihn auf sein Zimmer. Und noch desselben Tages empfing eine respektvoll erschütterte Welt die Nachricht von seinem Tode.

The location of the passage
The extract is the concluding lines of Thomas Mann's novelle, *Der Tod in Venedig*. Gustav von Aschenbach, the internationally respected man of letters, and Tadzio, the beautiful boy who is the object of his infatuation are almost the only people left on the hotel beach. Venice has been virtually abandoned by the tourists after an outbreak of Asiatic cholera. Their isolation underlines both the intensity of Gustav's feelings and the impossibility of his predicament.

A commentary on the passage
Tadzio is standing on a sand bar and is separated from his friends by a stretch of water. As he turns from the waist up, in an automatic, graceful movement and looks towards the shore, he mimics the figure of Hermes, the psychogogue and conductor of souls to the Underworld. There can be no reason for mistaking his shoreward glance. Aschenbach is being called. The way that the old man sits, watching Tadzio, recalls their first contact in the hotel, when their eyes had met for a very brief moment. Mann uses this parallel to underline the flimsiest of bases on which their relationship has been built up. On one level, a few glances and perhaps the odd smile have been enough to bring Aschenbach to the verge of destruction.

Gustav now follows Tadzio's movements with his eyes, as he has done frequently, throughout the tale. This in itself is symbolical of the character of their relationship. Tadzio is active, graceful youth, full of energy and movement. Gustav is venerable age and any involvement is purely vicarious.

When von Aschenbach lifts his head, as if in answer to Tadzio's gaze, we are again reminded that it is Tadzio who calls the tune. Gustav is in no position to act other than through infatuation and, once more, we are reminded how far he has descended from the self-discipline and control which had seen him through his career as an artistic writer.

While he thinks of the land of richest expectation to which the Tadzio-Hermes figure is pointing so irresistibly, his face has already taken on a relaxed and brooding look. It is a mask of death.

It is ironic, yet wholly appropriate, that it should take some little while for the hotel staff to realise that Gustav is dead and not merely sleeping. What more natural than that old age, confined to sitting and watching, while younger people act, should sit slumbering in the summer sun? The irony lies in the contrast between Gustav's quiescent exterior and his turbulent internal state of the last weeks.

There is further irony in the shock with which a respectful world learns of Gustav von Aschenbach's death. Such respect would soon have been dissipated, had his infatuation and self-destruction become public. How difficult it is to venerate an old man who chases round Venice after a pretty boy. One is left with the sad and abiding memory of an old man whose newly-dyed hair and made-up face have run, through the sweat of his own exertion as he chases after the boy to catch a glimpse of him. Old age cannot mask itself and pretend to be youth.

The significance of the passage
The passage marks the conclusion of Gustav von Aschenbach's descent from his position as a self-disciplined, venerated literary figure into the chaotic world of feelings and sensuality from which he had deliberately alienated himself in the early years of his artistic-literary career.

The way he quietly slumbers into death suggests that he has been worn out by the series of emotional crises he has undergone as a result of his fleeting contact with Tadzio. It is both fitting and ironic that Tadzio should recall the statue of a well-known figure of Classical Greek mythology, with which Gustav is more than familiar. In a sense, it is his own involvement in the world of art which has the last word. Gustav called to the Underworld by the human embodiment of a work of art, when it is his own final rejection of the relative security of a life immersed in art, which is his undoing.

The passage, and with it Gustav's final demise, present one outcome of a problem which is a major theme in Thomas Mann's work – the relationship between the artist and society. To an extent, Gustav von Aschenbach presents us with Tonio Kröger's predicament taken to its conclusion. Tonio, brought to feel with and for people again, makes the decision to re-isolate himself as the observer and interpreter of human kind, as the watcher outside the window. Gustav, so much older, had long been in the position, but there was enough of the emotional, the physical and the sensual left in him to destroy the precarious security brought about by total immersion in his art. Such may be the position of the artist in society.

Points of special interest

The dense quality of Thomas Mann's prose, the cumulative sentences, the hinted classical allusion, the quiet irony, all reflect the depths of the artist's problem. On one hand, there are vast resources of ability and perception, allied to the need to stand outside of humanity and observe, on the other, there is the need to feel and to be personally involved. This is the dilemma. Detachment provides a form of security. Emotional and physical relationships which go too deep do not.

This was the position of Thomas Mann's friend Gustav Mahler, the composer. In these final lines of *Der Tod in Venedig*, we are aware of how much of Mahler there is in the characterization of Gustav von Aschenbach.

Kattrin starrt in die Weite, auf die Stadt, und trommelt weiter.
DIE BÄUERIN *zum Alten:* Ich hab dir gleich gesagt, laß das Gesindel nicht auf den Hof. Was kümmerts die, wenn sie uns das letzte Vieh wegtreiben.
DER FÄHNRICH *kommt mit seinen Soldaten und dem jungen Bauern gelaufen:* Euch zerhack ich!
DIE BÄUERIN: Herr Offizier, wir sind unschuldig, wir können nix dafür, Sie hat sich raufgeschlichen. Eine Fremde.
DER FÄHNRICH: Wo ist die Leiter?
DER BAUER: Oben.
DER FÄHNRICH *hinauf:* Ich befehl dir, schmeiß die Trommel runter!
Kattrin trommelt weiter.
DER FÄHNRICH: Ihr seids alle verschworen. Das hier überlebt ihr nicht.
DER BAUER: Drüben im Holz haben sie Fichten geschlagen. Wenn wir einen Stamm holn und stochern sie herunter . . .
ERSTER SOLDAT *zum Fähnrich:* Ich bitt um Erlaubnis, daß ich einen Vorschlag mach. *Er sagt dem Fähnrich etwas ins Ohr. Der nickt.* Hörst du, wir machen dir einen Vorschlag zum Guten, Komm herunter und geh mit uns in die Stadt, stracks voran. Zeig uns deine Mutter, und sie soll verschont werden
Kattrin trommelt weiter.
DER FÄHNRICH *schiebt ihn roh weg:* Sie traut dir nicht, bei deiner Fresse kein Wunder. *Er ruft hinauf:* Wenn ich dir mein Wort gebe? Ich bin ein Offizier und hab ein Ehrenwort.
Kattrin trommelt stärker.
DER FÄHNRICH Der ist nix heilig.

The location of the passage

The extract is taken from the closing stages of Brecht's *Mutter Courage*, at the beginning of the siege of Halle. Kattrin is perched on a stable roof and is attempting to warn the citizens by beating a drum. She has only just begun and the Emperor's troops still have time to rescue the situation.

A commentary on the passage

The stage direction indicates that Kattrin is absorbed in her task. After a brief silence, the effect of the drumming on the audience is quite dramatic.

The reaction of the farmer's wife is both predictable and understandable. You must expect to find yourself in trouble, if you allow rabble like Kattrin and her mother, Courage, on the farm. They do not care about you and your problems. The Baüerin's comments provide an appropriate entry point for the ensign, whose first words show the blunt tactics that the military will employ. The farmers can expect no mercy from the soldiers, guilt or no guilt. Given the predicament in which the peasants find themselves, we cannot blame the Baüerin for fixing the blame for the drumming firmly where it belongs.

With typical lack of tact, the ensign attempts to bluster Kattrin into throwing down the drum. After the drama of his shouting, Kattrin's return to her drumming has a charged effect on the audience.

Typically, now that his blunt stratagem has not succeeded, the ensign threatens the farming family with death. Let them not think that they will survive this outrage. There is no time for niceties of behaviour. It is the Bauer, himself, who provides an intelligent, possible solution, when he suggests the use of a tree trunk to reach the roof.

It is now the turn of one of the squadees to make a suggestion, which is not so much subtle as devious. Let Kattrin come down, go to town with them, and they will spare her mother.

Kattrin's response is once more dramatic and, this time, strikes a chord of bathetic humour. Her drumming telegraphs the message to the audience, that no peasant in his or her right mind trusts anything the soldiers say. At this point, Brecht develops the possibility of a little humour. The ensign blames Kattrin's refusal to trust them on the soldier's 'ugly gob', a refusal with which he can sympathize. He believes he has the answer, by letting her know that he is an officer and therefore a man whose word is his bond. Kattrin's redoubled efforts on the drum are a fitting answer and, once more, are not lost on the audience.

The ensign's retort is highly ironic and reveals how the military and the peasants see war from two entirely different perspectives. When he states that nothing is sacred to her, he is clearly unaware that the common folk have just cause to trust nothing said by the military of either side in this festering war.

The significance of the passage
This is a highly dramatic passage, one of the functions of which is to prepare us for Courage's loss of yet another child. The emphasis is on activity, with much to-ing and fro-ing, a succession of short, sometimes pithy speeches and a great degree of tension. After the emotional involvement of this scene, the audience will be only too ready for the relative quiet and reflection of the final scene, in which Courage will sing her own, personal lament, before continuing determinedly on her way.

The scene is perhaps the most well-known in the play and it is significant that much important action occurs with Mother Courage off-stage. This underlines, if it needs underlining, the fact that it is her spirit and the strength of her presence which has helped so many people survive the rigours of years of warfare.

It is important also that the final scenes of the play should provide a strong ending. This Brecht achieves, not only by the combination of drama, tension, and humour which he provides in this passage, but by the device of involving us over the whole of a powerful scene in Courage's loss of a disabled daughter, whom she has protected from the moment we have known her. We have felt for Kattrin in her disabilities. Now, we feel for her, as we recognise her mother's spirit working in her. We are powerfully moved and ready for the conclusion of the play.

Points of special interest
The scene from which this extract is taken is an excellent example of a fundamental truth about Bertolt Brecht's best work. In plays such as *Mutter Courage, Galileo Galilei, Der Gute Mensch von Sezuan, Der kaukasische Kreidekreis*, there is much powerful emotion and the audience is fully involved. Where is the *Verfremdungseffekt* here?

This passage creates a considerable emotional response in the audience and catharsis is certainly functioning. The question we will always put and to which there can now be no answer, is how far did Brecht realise he had abandoned the *Verfremdungseffekt* theory in his best work?

11

The background essay

This type of essay has been introduced by certain Examination Boards in recent years and maintained by others over a much longer period in order to allow students some variety in the kinds of answers they write. Apart from providing a change, it is a deliberate attempt to help candidates of a less literary turn of mind, since it allows them to concentrate on the sociological and historical implications of specific books.

But the background essay should not be seen as a soft option. It has an intellectual rigour of its own and is as valid as the rest of the material on the paper.

There are two basic types of background essay. These are:

1 topics relating to important people, trends and events from the period studied.
2 Alternative topics of a non-literary nature on the actual set books.

EXAMPLE QUESTIONS

Type 1:
Discuss the contribution made by J. S. Bach, Ludwig Koch, Schopenhauer, Max von Laue or the Bauhaus to western society.
Type 2:
What do we learn of contemporary society from either *Grete Minde* or *Der Hauptmann von Köpenick*?

When we compare these two types of question, they appear to be looking for very different things. Type 1 seems to require something of a factual narrative on an historical basis, whereas Type 2 requires interpretation of material which you will have had to distil from a literary text.

If this apparent divergence were true, then the straightforward historical narrative would be an easier task than the interpretative analysis. In other words, students attempting Type 2 would be discriminated against, because they were choosing something which was intrinsically more demanding. But Examination Boards would not be foolish enough to allow such an unfair discrepancy. The truth is that Type 1 also requires some interpretation. Notice that the key word is *discuss*. It might well have been *analyse*.

TYPE 1 QUESTIONS

Let us look at sample paragraphs by two students who have written an essay on Max von Laue, in order to clarify the point.

A Max von Laue was a scientist of world repute, who worked with Einstein and Planck. He specialised in theoretical physics and won the Nobel Prize in 1914 at the relatively young age of 35. He remained an active scientist almost to his death at the age of 80 in 1960 and was at various times a professor at Frankfurt, Göttingen, and Berlin. In the course of his lifetime, he received a vast number of honours for his work, especially since he had given the world conclusive proof that matter really was constructed on an atomic basis. He was also something of a controversial figure politically. He spoke out against certain aspects of the Hitler regime on numerous occasions and, in 1957, warned against the German forces equipping themselves with atomic weapons.

B Max von Laue will long be remembered by society, not only for the great scientific advances which he achieved, but also for the humanitarian principles he brought to his work. Indeed, it would be a mistake to see his scientific endeavour and immense moral courage as separate strands in an individual's life, since they worked essentially in tandem.

His concern for humanity and justice made him speak out at no little personal risk in defence of Einstein and Fritz Haber at the time of their dismissal by the Nazi regime in the 1930's. In 1957, he was a strong voice among a group of highly prominent German scientists who spoke out against the provision of atomic weapons for the newly re-established German defence forces. Amongst his scientific achievements, his discoveries relating to X-ray light and the lattice-structure of crystals allowed massive advances to be made in the field of crystallography. He was essentially a theoretical physicist, who looked for practical applications of his discoveries wherever possible, because he was so aware of his responsibility to use his immense talent for the benefit of the human race as a whole.

It is easy to see why B will score much more highly than A. She has made a very worthwhile attempt to see beyond the basic facts and to assess their implications. There is real interpretation here. On the other hand, A has done little more than trot out a series of historical facts.

Thus, if you find yourself writing a background essay relating to historical or cultural developments, make sure you try to delve beneath the most obvious surface facts. A further paragraph taken from an essay describing the work of the artist, Max Beckmann, should help you to understand clearly what is expected of you, if you are to score well on this section of the paper.

C The temptation to classify Max Beckmann too precisely should be avoided. Although he is now the name most often quoted as typical of German Expressionism, this is an inaccurate stereotyping, since he belonged to no one school in isolation and was a leading light of neither *Die Brücke* nor *Der blaue Reiter*. Where he is very much an expressionist, is in the way he communicates what Herbert Read has called that 'metaphysical anxiety which is now the global condition of mankind.' Appropriately, much of his major work was provoked by personal and international disasters – the death of his mother in 1906, earthquakes, the sinking of the Titanic and his experiences of the Great War as a medical orderly, like Brecht, at the front line. The horror, misery and destruction he witnessed during this latter, lengthy disaster were to remain an abiding influence on his work.

This is a sound beginning to an essay and opens the way to discussion of the following points:

1 his reasons for his relative isolation
2 an analysis of the basis of Expressionism via the quotation
3 the influence of his mother
4 the effect of international events on the painter's vision
5 the influence of the Great War on Max Beckmann and others

The person writing a Type 1 essay will also set herself well on the way to success, if she proceeds to ask the following questions, which are a standard pattern to adopt, if the subject is concerned with a movement or a political/historical era:

1 Why did the phenomenon come about?
2 Were there parallels outside the main sphere of influence?
3 What caused its inevitable decline?
4 How, if at all, does it still affect our society?

CRUX QUESTIONS

Always try to answer whichever of the following questions are relevant to your topic:

1 Why did this event/phenomenon occur?
2 Why did this person come to prominence?
3 What are the (universal) implications for all of us?
4 Name any parallels in other countries or civilizations.
5 Why could the event/phenomenon (not) have occurred in your own country?
6 Why could the individual (not) have risen to prominence in your own country?
7 What lessons has the person/incident/movement/period taught us?

If you apply the above list to any Type 1 background question, it will automatically help your interpretation.

ASSIGNMENTS

1 Draw up a list of main points summarizing the achievements of any one or more of the following:

German Expressionism, the Bauhaus, the Berliner Ensemble, Bismarck, Konrad Adenauer, Willi Brandt, Heidi Kabel, Harald Schmid, Maria Schell, Heidi Genée, Dr. Veronica Carstens.

2 Draw up an essay plan, listing the main points relating to any ONE of the following:

> Junker élitism, the *Nullpunkt*, the Berlin–Blockade 1948, the Berlin Wall, the *Berufsverbot*.

TYPE 2 QUESTIONS

Background questions on specific literary texts have their own advantages and disadvantages. On the credit side, all the material on which you need to draw is contained within the compass of the set text you have studied.

Contrarily, this type of essay contains its own traps, since you are required to sift diligently among a mass of detail for items which are relevant to your socio-historical theme. Hence, the largest pitfall, about which we have already talked at length, looms large. With this type of essay, it can be especially difficult to avoid story-telling!

For many of these questions, there is an almost standard format, along the lines:

> What picture does X text give the reader of life/social problems/society, *at the time when the author was writing/in the . . . era?*

The word *picture* is the one to which you should pay special attention! *Picture* does not mean an interminable recounting of a scene or of events. Instead of looking for narrative sequences, concentrate on picking out informative details and on attempting a degree of interpretation. Ask yourself:

(a) *What do we learn about living conditions?* Is life easy/a struggle/calm/ frenzied/depressing/rewarding/superficial/meaningful, etc.?

(b) *What is the social environment like?* Are we presented with a uniform group of people/a mixed environment/a milieu which is culturally barren/ rich in characters/artistic/competitive/easy-going, etc.?

(c) *What is the prevailing atmosphere?* Is it progressive/repressive/energetic/ inert/hopeful/pessimistic?

(d) *How do people behave?* Are they (in)considerate/responsible/mean/hon-ourable/individualistic/cohesive/determined/apathetic?

(e) *What is the effect of recent events?* Is it stimulating/shattering/ruinous/ debilitating/regressive/encouraging?

(f) *What were communications like?* Were they rudimentary/improving/ newly mechanized/modern/advanced/non-existent?

(g) *How did people amuse themselves?* Independently/in groups/simply/so-phisticatedly/decently/immorally/cruelly?

(h) *What did they wear and have in their homes?* Is there evidence of different needs and aspirations/were people prevented from achieving anything more than a basic level of provision/is there great emphasis on posses-sions?

(j) *How was the political situation?* Was it complex/quiescent/dramatic/a time of change/historically most significant?

(k) *Is there evidence of the effect of war?* Is the prevailing atmosphere anxious/ fearful/one of relief? Is it a time of rebuilding/of major efforts to maintain the peace?

(l) *How did powerful individuals affect the environment?* Do real or fictional- ized figures of power enter the story? If not, are any referred to in passing? What insights do they offer into the corridors of power?

(m) *What lessons can we learn from looking into this part of the past?* Do the times related in the work reflect an era that was more peaceful/calm/ (un)just/aggressive/straightforward/stable?

If you apply the above list to any Type 2 question, it will help you to interpret automatically and to avoid story-telling. Use it to help you with the following practice exercises.

ASSIGNMENTS

Draw up essay plans for each of the following questions, relating it to one only of your set books. You need list only the main points.

1 What picture does the text give the reader of contemporary social problems?
2 What impressions does the reader gain of contemporary society from the work?
3 How accurately does the work reflect the political times in which it was written?
4 In what ways does the society presented differ radically from our own?

12

Examination revision and technique

REVISION

You will already have come across some suggestions to help you with your revision in Chapter 4. They and the hints below are all based on the premise that it is possible to prepare yourself reasonably fully for most questions on a text without reading the whole of the book again in the last weeks preceding your examination. Although it is a good idea in principle to read right through a work when revising, in reality you often just do not have the time.

Don't worry too much about this, since there is nothing like a shortage of time to concentrate the mind! If you have made good notes on a book (see pages 37–9), you will be able to read through it quite quickly, searching out the main details and spending more time on the more significant sections.

Always bear the exam in mind when you start studying a new text. Highlight significant passages by underlining, or by a line down the margin. Make marginal notes relating to themes and to character traits, etc. When you come across points of repetition or of contrast, reminding you of something which has occurred some pages back, make a reference in the margin of both pages.

THE SCRAP-BOOK

Keep a *scrap-book* of newspaper and magazine items which have any relevance at all to the books you are studying. The cuttings may be critical reviews of a new book by or about one of your authors, a film notice dealing with a similar theme to that of one of your set texts, or a picture of life in Germany, confirming, or contrasting with, a point your author has made. The cutting may even be something as simple as a photo of a place associated with one of your authors.

What is the use of such a scrap-book, especially for exam revision?

Remember that literature essays give you the opportunity to show more than a suitably detailed knowledge and understanding of a text. If you can reveal, in addition to these essentials, some awareness of the author and of his or her life, this will give you credit in the form of marks. More important, you will have earned the credit, because you will have achieved something worthwhile. You will probably have discovered some of the wider implications of that author for yourself.

In the same way, German films which deal with themes similar to those treated in your set texts, will once again act as a point of reference or of comparison. A small amount of such comparison in your essays will telegraph to the examiner your ability to draw parallels with things outside the text, which is one indication of a literate and lively mind.

Your scrap-book will be particularly useful when you are revising before your exam, since you will have set it out in a bright and thematic way. Your mind will retain much of the basic information in it, since colourful detail is something onto which the memory can latch with ease. Additionally, a scrap-book becomes something very personal and items from it included in your exam answers will have several advantages. Firstly, they will tend to transmit an impression of your own, *personal* enthusiasm in a way in which statements like 'Anna Seghers is a great author because . . .' never can. Secondly, some of the information will be much more up to date than, say, the background notes contained in the particular edition of the text which you happen to be using. Thirdly, and perhaps most importantly, because the details have come from items which you have selected for your scrap-book, they will be different from the material written by your neighbour and may even be sufficiently individual for you to stand out from the thousands of other candidates sitting the exam around the country. It is this individuality which may eventually mark out your work as something special.

ADDITIONAL SOURCES OF SCRAP-BOOK MATERIALS

Remember that you are entitled to single photocopies of small extracts from published works, provided they are genuinely for personal study.

You might photocopy photographs and drawings from social history books of the period, pages showing historical parallels with England, examples of work by contemporary artists, small sections from literary histories (such as the Ullstein series) and *occasional* comments by literary critics.

EXAM QUESTION PREPARATION

A favourite summer-time occupation is question-spotting! At some time or other, most of us will have been guilty of poring over lists of past questions to try to guess precisely which questions on a set author will come up.

This is a dangerous activity similar to Russian roulette and not just because you may swot up the wrong questions! Even if the right one does appear on the paper, you may still have actually done yourself a disservice by banking on it, since other, alternative questions may have been easier or more exploitable, had you kept an open approach.

You are being advised not to look for *banker questions*. What else can you do to give yourself a good start in the exam room?

There are strategies you can follow which will allow you a wide spread of preparation, to the extent that any essay can be half-written in your mind *before* you start the exam (see pages 38–9).

Although you have been advised not to look for a single question, you can still be fairly certain of the types of question that may be asked. The basic essay types are:

1 Character studies
2 Themes and implications
3 Success or failure/strengths or weaknesses of the work
4 Implications for you
5 Style/characteristic features
6 General appeal
7 How the work fits into a pattern or literary movement
8 Structure of the work.

Very understandably, you will be thinking, 'Eight basic types of essay! How can I prepare all those and still have a clear idea of part of my essay before I even enter the room?'

Read through the advice on pages 36–40 again. Even if you cannot, or are not prepared to, learn gradually and systematically a series of quotations from each book, you can identify a mixture of 20–30 crucial passages in the text, to which you can refer specifically without giving the author's exact words.

Next, go back to the list of the basic types of essay. Now that you have a fresh picture in your mind of the more important passages within the work, go through each type from character study to structure and think out for yourself which individual touches, events, traits will be relevant to which type of question. Gradually, you will be able to practise this at any time without any books in front of you. As you become used to the list and to working with it, you will be able to rehearse almost any standard question which is likely to occur. When, finally, you are confronted with the exam situation, your confidence should be greater since you will have practised the themes that crop up. Equally importantly, because of this training, you will recognize more quickly than many candidates the implications of particular questions: which are more straightforward or difficult, which suit your particular attitude to the work, which are best avoided. You will weigh up the situation more quickly and will be much more likely to make the best choice for yourself, since you will not have restricted yourself by preparing and praying for the home banker.

ASSIGNMENTS

1 In each of your set texts identify 30 crucial passages and/or quotations.
2 For each of your set texts, note the passages relevant to each basic essay type.
3 If you are in the early or middle stages of your German course, start a literature scrap-book *now*.

EXAM TECHNIQUE

As soon as you have your exam paper in front of you:

(a) Read through the questions on *all* your authors, before starting to write.

(b) Decide which questions you are going to answer.
(c) Decide the order in which you will answer, starting with your strongest and ending with your weakest title.
(d) Write a brief plan for each essay before you start to write the essay proper.
(e) Apportion your time correctly, i.e. if the exam is three hours long and you have four questions to answer, try to allow $\frac{3}{4}$ hour for each, unless your last is sufficiently weak that part of its time is better given to the other three.
(f) Keep watching the time to make sure you follow your schedule. If there is not likely to be a central clock, make sure you take a watch to the exam room.
(g) Keep checking what you write against the title, to avoid digression.
(h) Include a reasonable amount of quotation in your answers, if at all possible.
(i) Make sure you give each essay a definite conclusion, so that it does not simply peter out.

ASSIGNMENTS

1 Obtain one of your Examination Board's past papers, decide before you look at it on which author you intend to write an answer, shut yourself away for the stipulated time, write an essay and hand it to your teacher/lecturer for comment. Do not look at any books while you are attempting this exercise.
2 Now do the same for a full past paper, in one sitting.

EXAM ESSAY PLANS (see also Chapter 3)

Because of pressure of time, you will not be in a position to draw up as detailed a plan as with a normal essay done in term or holiday time. The essentials to incorporate in your attenuated plan are:

(a) a one-line statement of each main point
(b) a list of items to be included in your introduction
(c) brief notes on your conclusion
(d) quotes to be included.

Below is an example of how such a plan might look. You will see that it does contain the important material, which is set out clearly enough to allow the candidate to write a logical, smooth-flowing answer. Once again, do not fall into the trap of spending as long on your plan as on the writing of the actual essay.

Try to make sure that you produce a plan of some sort before you start the draft on which you are to be assessed. People who cannot be bothered to draw up an initial outline of their essay tend to end up writing a composition which *looks* as if they cannot be bothered. With a little planning, you will have made a good start towards producing something worthwhile.

ESSAY TITLE: Discuss the tragic method employed by Schiller in 'Maria Stuart'.

MAIN POINTS: 1. Retrospective analysis. Audience privileged to be in the

Mein Schicksal   seats of the Gods. Soon presented with the ironies of

liegt in meiner   history. *Under lined by the fact that,*

Feinde Hand

Er wird nimmer 2. "Very early on, Maria is aware of what is likely to happen

Friede mit mir   to her."

machen Bis meines

Unglücks Maß

erfüllet ist

　　　　　　　　3. Our attention directed to the final stages of her tragedy.

Perhaps Mention: 4. Implicit in the tragedy, Schiller's preoccupation with the

S. has been hard on   questions of freedom and moral grace.

Elisabeth.

Mention also: Com-

pression of time. 5. Liberties taken with historical accuracy. Queens made

Meeting between 2   much younger to increase poignancy and appeal.

queens never took

Place

　　　　　　　　6. Various devices to maintain a high level of dramatic

　　　　　　　　　 tension: *Doch zog ich strenge Königspflichten vor*

　　　　　　　　　　　 Und doch gewann sie aller Männer Gunst.

　　　　　　　　 —contrast of two queens' 'Weltanschauungen'

　　　　　　　　 —Maria often impervious to helpful suggestions

Sie führt den Blitz,

sie ist die königin, —Kennedy as the voice of reason

Vor Ihrem Buhlen

habt Ihr sie ver-

höhnt!

　　　　　　　　 —Emotional charge of the confession

　　　　　　　　 —Appeals to audience's sense of justice

Sagt ihr ——→—Maria's magnanimity at execution

Daß ich ihr meinen

Tod von ganzem

Herzen vergebe

CONCLUSION: Schiller skilfully leaves us with disarray among Maria's ill-

　　　　　　　　 wishers. Maria vindicated by way Shrewsbury abandons

　　　　　　　　 Elisabeth. + *even worse, Leicester has flown!*

　　　　　　　　 Verzeih, ich bin zu alt Und diese grade Hand, sie ist

　　　　　　　　 zu starr, Um deine neuen Taten zu versiegeln.

13

Your own errors of style

If you are not happy with your essay style, there is a lot you can do to improve it quickly. The best way to start is to find a composition that you have already written, or, preferably, several such compositions, and to look for characteristic weaknesses in the ideas you have produced and the way you have expressed them. Most of your difficulties will be found in the list below.

BAD SPELLING

This particular blemish is mentioned first, partly because most of us are prone to it, and partly because it is a serious fault about which this book can do nothing, other than to point out the obvious. It is a blemish with which one can sympathize, because of the highly irregular nature of English spelling. Sympathy is not, however, enough, since for people writing literature essays, standards are high. It is unquestionably right that they should be so, as a glance at the two versions of the same paragraph below will confirm:

A To a curtain extent, the characters of Bärlach and Gastmann cymbelise the forces of Good and Evill. It would therefor be a reasonnable asumption to see there behaviour as allways polariced. But, if we look carefuly at the evidence in 'Der Richter und sein Henker', we see that the two oponents do not totaly fullfill our expectations.

B To a certain extent, the characters of Bärlach and Gastmann symbolise the forces of Good and Evil. It would therefore be a reasonable assumption to see their behaviour as always polarised. But, if we look carefully at the evidence in 'Der Richter und sein Henker', we see that the two opponents do not totally fulfil our expectations.

The first version of the above paragraph was submitted by a student in his first year in the Sixth Form. The lesson is an obvious one for us, when we can recognize easily the spelling mistakes of others. We find it difficult to treat seriously what the essayist is saying, because the glaring errors intrude on our concentration and cause either irritation, or, as in the case of *curtain, cymbelise, polariced*, possible mirth, which can be an even more damaging reaction than irritation.

If you yourself are not a good speller and do not make a determined effort to check the sort of words you know you get wrong, then you are likely to provoke the same sort of reaction in your readers as Paragraph A above.

This is a great pity. If we reflect on the correctly spelt version, we will see that the writer is making a perfectly valid point. He has clearly thought about his topic and has made a definite statement, which is worth the writing. It is a shame that his spelling undermines both his status and his credibility with us.

The moral is obvious. If you cannot spell, keep a dictionary by your side when you write. More important still, consult it whenever you are not sure of a spelling.

ASSIGNMENT

Turn to page 104 and complete Exercise A.

VAGUE OR IMPRECISE EXPRESSION

This is another difficult fault to correct, since it is not always easy to realize that you have committed it. One of the basic problems in writing a literature essay is the fact that you have to be far more precise than in ordinary conversation.

When you are talking to people, you can half-refer to things, leave sentences unfinished, rely on gestures, simply because your listeners will often be well aware of the situation about which you are talking and will only need to sift a few pieces of information from the words you use.

But when you are tackling an essay, beware of bringing your conversational habits to your literary style. Avoid writing unfinished ideas, partial analogies, incomplete references, careless syntax, as in:

> It is obviously through Keller's observation of such a society, which draws him to expose the underlying character.

ASSIGNMENT

Turn to page 104 and complete Exercise B.

LOOSE OR SLANG EXPRESSION

Again, this is a failing which you may have to make an effort to eradicate, since (a) it is so easy to fall into, (b) loose expression is often acceptable in conversation. The trouble is that, used in essays, it will irritate the reader and will stop you presenting your ideas accurately, since most colloquial expression is an approximation:

> Mörike, like a lot of Romantic poets, was a *bit of a loner*. Andersch has a *fantastic* feel for the period. Impersonal authority succeeds in *putting the frighteners* on K and Joseph K.

The italicized items in the examples above jar on the reader, and, more importantly, give less information than other choices of expression might have done.

ASSIGNMENT

Turn to page 105 and complete Exercise C.

CLICHÉ

Cliché is a close relation of loose expression. A cliché is a hackneyed expression which has lost its effectiveness and colour over the years through over-use. Phrases such as *carrying coals to Newcastle, black as night* are often quoted as examples. Such statements have almost no real meaning, since they trip so readily out of the brain and off the tongue that we do not think about them. They therefore indicate a lack of original thought. Think carefully when you are about to use one of these all-purpose formulae in a sentence and find an alternative in your own words. Judge for yourself how watered-down the effect of the language is in the example below:

> Taugenichts wanders through the countryside *free as a bird* and eventually finds *the love of his life*.

ASSIGNMENT

Turn to page 105 and complete Exercise D.

INVOLVED WRITING

If, writing long sentences, in the course of which you employ many intricately linked subordinate clauses, the relationship between which is not always clear, and if, in so doing, you involve the reader in the tedious exercise of sifting through to determine exactly what is being said, you cause extreme irritation and, worse, fail to communicate to him the focus of your thoughts, so that it would be hardly surprising if you were to alienate him from an essay, which, had it not been for the involved expression, might have contained much that was worth the saying.

The last sentence should have made the point clearly!

In general, sentences should be varied both in length and in the way you begin them. Try not to write too many which are more than four lines long. Also, you should avoid starting each one with the subject and verb. Here is an example of an involved sentence taken from an A-level essay:

> Irony is a form of tangential comment displaying the discrepancy between the real (Sein) and the ostensible (Schein), through which the reader is placed in the privileged position of being able to determine that which is *Sein* and that which is *Schein*, thereby extracting possible humour from the discrepancy as well as regarding the plot with prescience and hindsight.

What did that sentence mean? Perhaps, but only perhaps, it may have been developing the following line of thought:

> Irony is a form of indirect comment, which reveals the discrepancy between a real and an apparent situation. Frequently, the reader is in the privileged position of knowing what has happened or what is to happen in the work. Thus, she can work out that discrepancy for herself and see its potential, humorous or otherwise.

Whether or not the last paragraph is a correct interpretation is irrelevant. It is not the reader's job to sort out exactly what the writer means.

ASSIGNMENT

Turn to page 105 and complete Exercise E.

REPETITION

This is one of the commonest faults, for the reasons outlined elsewhere. Fortunately, it is also one of the easiest to eliminate. To establish the effect on the reader of excessive repetition, analyse your own reaction to the following paragraph:

> Günther Grass is a realistic author with a very direct style. In his novels, he uses very realistic language, including obscenities which could offend because they are so direct. I, personally, do not find the obscenities offend me, since they are part of his artistic method in an attempt to achieve a sense of realism. In a sense, anyone who appreciates his artistic style and motivation, would not find the language obscene in the artistic sense of the word.

Although the writer has clearly been unaware of repeating himself, you, the reader, will have noticed several examples and your mind, instead of following the flow of the ideas, will have stopped to make the wrong sort of observations. The mind searches for a little variety in what it reads.

If you have a tendency towards unnecessary repetition, you can start to help yourself immediately, by looking back through previous essays, paragraph by paragraph. Where you spot examples of this blemish, pencil in alternative expressions.

ASSIGNMENT

Turn to page 106 and complete Exercise F.

OVER-VERBALIZATION

Over-verbalization is a good name for this fault, since its very ugliness gives us a clue to its nature. It is the use of over-long, over-complex words and phrases to render situations which could have been expressed much more simply.

This sin usually occurs when people are trying to impress through the use of long words. It may be a result of over-exposure to zealous radio and television presenters, commentators and critics.

Whatever the reasons for it, if your prose contains a large number of long words, go back to the Anglo-Saxon!

The English language has two levels. Our basic survival vocabulary relating to everyday needs is Anglo-Saxon (e.g. eat, drink, sleep, awaken, bread, butter, flesh, blood), but our intellectual language, that of the courts, both legal and regal, is either Latin or French, which in itself is vulgar Latin (e.g. sentiment, discourse, entreaty, significance, sentence). If what we have written has ended up as something rather pompous or 'high-falutin', then, almost certainly, it will contain a high percentage of originally Latin (and Greek) vocabulary:

> Franz Kafka is quintessentially the writer of the dispossessed, as may be deduced from a total opus so redolent of Angst, Weltschmerz and personal trauma, that one perceives a nascent sado-masochistic symbiosis developing between the oppressor and the oppressed.

> Franz Kafka's overriding concern is with the dispossessed. This comes across clearly in all his work, which is so full of anxiety, fear and pain. There also seems to be a mutual dependence developing between the oppressors who inflict the pain and the oppressed who suffer it.

The alternative is much easier to understand because it attempts to express a complex situation simply. The elements *quintessentially, opus, redolent, Angst, Weltschmerz, trauma, nascent, sado-masochistic* and *symbiosis* have been substituted by much more straightforward vocabulary.

This is not to say that words such as *opus, nascent, Angst* have no place in the literary essay. Quite the opposite. Such language is totally appropriate, provided it is used sparingly. A large number of big words in one sentence will usually be too much for the brain to take. Besides, it will sound highly artificial.

ASSIGNMENT

Turn to page 107 and complete Exercise G.

PADDING

This blemish is endemic in most, if not all, essayists. For most of us, it remains below the surface, until we are called upon to write on a topic of which our knowledge is scanty or superficial. Then, we tend to fill out our paragraphs with irrelevant ideas and illustrations, and, most commonly, with woolly or background statements introduced at random to cover a lack of something to say.

Padding can be at least partly avoided with a little courage and by taking the following steps:

1 Keep looking back at the title of your essay.
2 Avoid frequent use of long sentences.

3 Introduce relevant quotations.
4 Comment specifically on these.
5 Avoid overloading your essay with background information.
6 Avoid guessing at possible links between points.
7 Refrain from introducing side-issues.

EXERCISES

A   SPELLING

Correct the spelling, where necessary:

(a) Here, Böll puts his comitment into practise.
(b) The novel ends with the fulfillment of the prophesy.
(c) Andersch's perpose cannot posibly be missinterpreted.
(d) Many of Brecht's plays are a reflecsion of terbulent times.
(e) Her work is both fasinating and purturbing.
(f) The arguement has not been developped logicaly.
(g) The play procedes to a definate climax.
(h) In much of the work of Grass, there is a curtain agressive quality.
(i) The forgoing pasage is an example of this.
(j) She fails in her atempt to divine the truth.
(k) Their is a lesson to be percieved.

B   VAGUE EXPRESSION AND BAD SYNTAX

Tighten or correct each of the following:

(a) In our capacity as observers, their lack of awareness of the outcome is tragic.
(b) By writing *Sansibar*, affirms this commitment to humanity.
(c) Zweig is a compassionate author. He sees people as they are.
(d) Here we see one more aspect of Brecht's political stand which is obvious.
(e) Another aspect of the work which impresses by its accuracy, is that of background.
(f) Brecht's plays have a complex style. They are difficult.
(g) The two plays are a pair.
(h) Thomas Mann connotates irony through his language.
(i) Goethe achieves an artistic whole.
(j) He thinks of the girl in the next room, a soldier returning after the war.
(k) It is obviously through Keller's observation of such a society which drove him to expose this underlying character.
(l) This reveals her sarcasm of the middle classes.
(m) Anna Seghers is a communist writer. She is committed to it.

C POPULAR AND SLANG EXPRESSION

Rewrite these sentences in a more suitable style:

(a) Gustav von Aschenbach makes a mint out of his artistic endeavours.
(b) You get the feeling that Dürrenmatt allows Bärlach to be on a hiding to nothing.
(c) *Der Mann mit den Messern* takes the lid off life in Germany at the end of the war.
(d) *Die Dame am Steuer* drives like a maniac.
(e) Taugenichts is living on a perpetual high.
(f) Eventually, it all gets up Joseph K's nose.
(g) Karl-Heinz needs a bit of a jump-start to get him going.
(h) The hero has got ants in his pants.
(i) The meeting is pretty traumatic.
(j) Whether she does it is six and two threes.
(k) Egmont has to take a lot of hammer from Alba.
(l) Grete's lot is not a happy one.
(m) Predictably, Jochen gets in a right twist.
(n) Ludwig's behaviour hits an all-time low.
(o) The story is a bit of a tear-jerker.

D CLICHÉ AND NOTHING-STATEMENTS

(a) Christa Wolf has an ability for getting right to the heart of the matter.
(b) The inspector is on the spot as quick as lightning.
(c) Reinhardt Mey sings like a nightingale.
(d) Katya is a Mother-Earth figure.
(e) Udo has more feeling in his little finger, than all the others put together.
(f) In the army, Greck is a fish out of water.
(g) Karl is as sadistic as the devil himself.
(h) Their ultimate happiness is never really threatened, since love conquers all.
(i) The Jewess is spared because she has the voice of an angel.
(j) The atmosphere is so tense, that one's heart is in one's mouth.
(k) Benno would be well advised to look before he leaps.
(l) Hölderlin has an incredible capacity for language.
(m) Thomas Mann uses a lot of imagery.

E INVOLVED WRITING

Re-write the following so they may be understood. In each case, you may use several shorter sentences.

(a) Thomas Mann's style in *Der Tod in Venedig* may rightly be described as dense, on account of his predilection for symbol, classical allusions, extended allegory and erudition, as a means of conveying not only the artist's predicament, but the complex inter-relationship between the intellectual, spiritual and physical worlds which the non-artist, normally unaware of the conflicting forces to which the artistic personality is prey, may, himself, devine from time to time through the pen of the writer-seer.

(b) To me, Goethe's poetry is important, not simply for its lyricism, its innovation, its energy and its imagery, but for the statement it provides, at times definitive, of the end of an era and of the beginning of the Modern Age, as perceived by a man of exceptional feeling and intellect with a natural tendency towards iconoclasm and who makes conscious use of his revolutionary fervour and empathy for mankind, a synthesis which is at least hinted at by his outburst in 'Prometheus'.

(c) Whether Anna Seghers may be regarded as a truly universal writer, depends on the reader's assessment of the political perspective in her work, and whether her admiration for Eastern European socialism and her criticism of what might be termed the decadent right, themes which are frequently present in her work, are presented with sufficient moderation so as not to obscure the more universal qualities, such as the breadth of her view of human nature and her ability to present the essence of a situation and to allow the Western reader to feel that she is much more than an East German writer, simply writing for an East German public.

(d) If we are to ask ourselves what is the basis of Christa Wolf's own, particular art, then we are setting ourselves a task requiring precise and sensitive analysis, since she is a writer whose method is often exceptionally subtle and whose delineation of apparently life-like situations in which the reader's disbelief is suspended, depends on what we might term the concealment of art, which may, itself, rely principally on devices such as understatement and the use of gentle humour.

F   REPETITION

Wherever possible, find alternatives for unnecessary repetitions:

(a) Stefan Zweig's strength lies in psychological character description. He is a psychologist, who provides strong descriptions of his characters.
(b) Probably, we have here the probable motive.
(c) This observation shows her skill as an observer.
(d) Presuming this to be the case, we presume it is a reflection of his background.
(e) This is actually the first occasion on which he occasions actual bodily harm.
(f) She has an eye for detail. She is influenced by her memories of childhood. She uses these to provide a series of cameos.

(g) This sensitivity allows for sensitive description, since this author's purpose in this work is to describe states of mind.

(h) It is at this level that we understand the level to which she has sunk.

(i) He considers alternatives, such as considering himself to be the devil's representative.

(j) She is a perceptive author, who perceives the essence of the human predicament.

G OVER-VERBALIZATION

Simplify the complex expression of the following:

(a) Because of the artful simplicity of her prose, the author elicits a maximised cathartic response.

(b) The reader, the vicarious observer, is the quintessential watcher at the window of transient experience.

(c) Such a character, who touches his nadir in a welter of nihilistic response, is anathema to us.

(d) How are we to extrapolate the nucleus, when the author has such a predilection for obscurantism?

(e) The essence of the author-reader relationship is a prototypal symbiosis.

(f) The author's eclecticism finds its apogee in her delineation of ambiance and milieu.

(g) Craft has shaped the novel to correspond diametrically to the hiatus in the protagonist's career.

(h) Despite the character's percipience, his Schadenfreude is not a reliable parameter for action.

H GRAMMATICAL INACCURACY

Correct the grammar as required in the sentences below:

(a) Zuckmayer is one of those dramatists who has left a mark on the twentieth century.

(b) Between Greta and he, there was no understanding.

(c) Heine's sensitivity and musicality springs immediately to mind.

(d) There are less characters who are believable, than in her previous work.

(e) With the years, the picture becomes more clearer.

(f) The fleeing soldiers were caught and hung from posts.

(g) Anna Seghers is an author for who she had a great respect.

(h) No one have a sharper idea of evil than Dürrenmatt.

(i) There is too many themes in the work.

(j) Writing all his books, she was the mainstay of his support.

Sample essay

The essay was written under examination conditions and reflects the standard expected of a very good candidate at A-level.

How far do you agree with the view that Andersch's novel, "Sansibar oder der letzte Grund" is an essentially optimistic work?

Sansibar oder der letzte Grund reflects the very real struggles of many men and women of goodwill in Germany and its occupied territories before and during the Second World War. The novel, itself, is very clearly optimistic in the sense that the humanitarian objectives of the dangerous boat-journey are achieved. Both Judith, the young Jewess, and Barlach's wooden sculpture, *der Lesende Klosterschüler*, symbol of the freedom of thought so inimical to the Nazi movement, are eventually ferried to safety in neutral Sweden. But, the goal is achieved at some cost and the future of those protagonists who will return with the boat to Germany is uncertain. Optimistic one may be, but the battle between the forces of good and evil will always be closely run. In the words of Gregor:

Alles muß neu geprüft werden.

Andersch's novel is a work of committed literature with an unambiguous message. From seemingly average people confronted with a frightening crisis, we discern patterns of behaviour and human solidarity, which raise them above the pettiness of so much of the human condition. The lesson really is that most people have within them the innate strength and positive qualities to overcome evil, if they will only allow themselves to act according to the better side of their nature.

This is shown clearly by the way in which the major characters, drawn from a variety of backgrounds to symbolise the universality of their problems, mature, and lose some of their prejudices in the course of events. We recognise this process in Knudsen, when his antipathy towards Gregor diminishes. He begins to understand the young official from the ZK and even to understand his position:

vielleicht müssen die Jüngeren so kneifen wie er. Wenn die Partei schon im Eimer ist, dann müssen die Jungen so kneifen wie er, und die Älteren wie ich.

This is a considerable admission for a middle-aged man, set in his ways.

Knudsen has previously blamed Central Committee officialdom for the failure of the Communist Party to bring change in Germany. What is significant, is not the actual change in his attitudes, but the fact that middle age is no bar to positive thought. Circumstances can act to eliminate our prejudices.

It is difficult to say who undergoes the most change in *Sansibar*. What can be said with certainty, is that all of the main characters change for the better. Judith, like so many of the oppressed minorities of Europe at this time, has had to grow up in a matter of days. Gregor sees this reflected in her face:

> ... es hatte nun alle Verwöhntheit verloren, es war ein frierendes bleiches Nachtgesicht geworden, ein unsicheres Gesicht.

Thus, a great cause for optimism in Andersch's characters is the fact that they are able to adapt to circumstances. The process will be a painful one, but they will come through.

Of none is this more true than of Pfarrer Helander. Ironically, Andersch has his elderly clergyman make the biggest sacrifice, that of his life. But, the term 'sacrifice' is a misnomer. His death is a form of 'Freitod', which he makes for his God, and to protect life in the future:

> Wie dumm von mir, dachte der Pfarrer, zu denken, ich schösse, um Gott zu züchtigen. Gott läßt mich schießen, *weil er das Leben liebt.*

These last words are crucial to an understanding of the novel. In *Sansibar*, the pulse of life beats strongly, whether it is Christian, Jewish, agnostic, or atheist. Nazism is anti-life. It is a challenge to which the main protagonists rise and which they must defeat. How fitting, that Helander, in all his sickness and near death, should strike a blow for freedom.

There is, of course, great irony in the way in which Helander makes his commitment. It is the man of God, the man of peace, who cleaves to violence as an immediate solution. He shoots first at 'die Anderen', to protect 'den Klosterschüler', his own integrity and the future of those around him. There is a clear indication here, that Good will sometimes have to resort to violence to overcome Evil. Nazism and 'die Anderen' are Evil personified:

> So also sieht das Gesindel aus: Fleisch in Uniformen, Teiggesichter unter Hüten.

The individual who provides perhaps the most important key to an interpretation of the novel and to an understanding of the nature of Andersch's optimism, is 'der Junge'. Significantly, the novel both starts and finishes with him. Additionally, we never know his real name. To us, he is always 'der Junge', for he is to symbolise youth.

Of all the individuals, it is he who does the most growing in the course of the work. Helander accepts his own 'Freitod' with little of his life left before him. 'Der Junge', with the possibility of many years to come, rejects Sansibar, the golden land, and opts to return to Germany, where danger and death lurk. He has made the choice for himself, and, on his youthful decision to take up the good fight, if only by simply being there, hangs Andersch's cause for optimism in the future of mankind.

Typically, his decision is neither made nor greeted with any great fuss. There is a life to be lived, in which freedom may be fought for and will be re-achieved, only to be guarded in the future by eternal vigilance:

> Der Junge blickte nicht mehr in den Wald zurück, als er den Steg betrat. Er schlenderte auf das Boot zu, als sei nichts geschehen.

A Glossary of literary terms

The *Biedermeier* literature of the later years of the nineteenth century is a direct reflection of the political and social changes engineered by amongst others, Otto von Bismarck. It coincides with the growth of the Bürgertum and is comfortable, bourgeois and inward-looking. Its themes tend to be parochial, with a deliberate avoidance of international and universal issues.

The *Bildungsroman* is the novel of character development and is a major German genre. In such a work, an individual is seen to progress through various stages of immaturity to a greater strength of character, understanding of his/her own position, etc. By the very nature of the exercise, such works tend to be lengthy. Examples of the best-known *Bildungsromane* are *Wilhelm Meisters Lehrjahre*, *Der grüne Heinrich* and *Der Zauberberg*.

Die Brücke and *Der Blaue Reiter* are artistic groupings within German Expressionism (q.v.), in which Impressionism was seen as excessively passive and refined and as consequently irrelevant to a discordant society. The artists involved in *Die Brücke* and *Der Blaue Reiter* were, above all, highly articulate, experimental and radical. They represent a strong movement away from the representational and their work is often characterized by a deliberately harsh, garish use of colour.

Classicism   Greek art and literature are taken as a model for the writer. There is a consequent emphasis on purity of form and expression.

German Expressionism is part of a literary and artistic revolution, which began before 1900 and was given particular impetus by the horrors of the Great War. The Movement is aggressively outspoken against a system which can produce such horrors and reacts against the idea of man and woman as central figures in a stable universe, by presenting the chaos it has perceived.

Der Kahlschlag/Die Gruppe 47/der Nullpunkt/Heimkehrliteratur/Trümmerliteratur are all terms relating to a group of writers who gave German literature a new start after the disasters of the Second World War. Their work is characterised by a sense of responsibility for and towards society, by the use of straightforward, non-literary language and by extreme honesty in their choice of themes and material.

The Mutter Erde (the Earth Mother/Mother Earth) is a motif which has been prominent in German literature since the Middle Ages. The *Mutter Erde* figure in a modern work will be a female character who will symbolize the maternal virtues of dependability, emotional strength and physical warmth, predominantly in relation to male characters who turn to her for shelter, consolation, or plain succour.

Naturalism was the late nineteenth-century literary movement based on the doctrine that the writer's art should combine the faithful observation and reproduction of nature with a form of scientific method. Hence, characters within a work are seen to be the product of their own heredity and environment.

Neue Sachlichkeit (the *New Objectivity*) is a relatively short-lived movement in the German Arts, most in evidence during the few apparently stable years of the Weimar Republic (approx. 1925–1930/2). This form of neo-realism shows a determination to portray accurately, contemporary German society. With the deepening economic and social crisis, its adherents became increasingly left-of-centre and developed a philosophy which became known as 'white socialism'.

Realism arose out of the belief that Art should be a sincere and true reflection of reality. Life was to be reproduced with meticulous accuracy and there was a consequent strong dislike of such devices as exaggeration, idealisation, extreme coincidence. *Naturalism* (q.v.) is an extreme development of Realism.

German Romanticism is almost impossible to define both accurately and completely. In Romantic literature, the spirit, rather than reason, is predominant. The heart is taken as a better guide to the condition of the individual and of society than are scientific and industrial progress, and the writer will often be looking for a synthesis between *Natur* and *Geist*.

The *Sturm und Drang* (also known as *Die Geniezeit*) was a period in German literature (approx. 1767–1787) characterised by a youthful, energetic radicalism. Reactionary forces in literature and in the social order were shaken and sometimes destroyed by the wealth of new ideas propounded by writers of exceptional vitality and talent. Chief amongst these were Herder, the young Goethe, and Schiller.

Surrealism was an artistic and literary movement of the 1920s and 30s which reacted against the violent and absurd nature of society by producing art which was itself often violent, absurd and dream-like, reflecting in particular the influence of Freud's theory of dreams.

The *Wille zum Tode* (the death-wish)   Like *Mutter Erde* (q.v.), this phenomenon has been identifiable in German literature from the Middle Ages. A character who is said to have a death-wish follows a pattern of behaviour which may be seen as self-destructive and may appear to provoke his/her own demise. The concept of the death-wish has been validated in relatively recent times through the work of Sigmund Freud and other psychiatrist-researchers. Consequently, the motif of the *Wille zum Tode* is found in modern literature as well as in its precursor.

Answers to assignments

Chapter 1, page 10: Assignment
    (a) pathetic   (b) highly charged   (c) joyful   (d) sinister
    (e) despairing   (f) full of suspense

Chapter 2, page 21: Assignment
    (a) 3 direct and staccato   (b) 1 optimistic   (c) 4 epic
    (d) 1 official, formal   (e) 1 part sympathetic, part ironic
    (f) 4 whimsical   (g) 3 optimism   (h) 2 imply character
    (i) 2 contrasting   (j) 1 build the tension

Chapter 13, page 104: Spelling
    (a) commitment, practice   (b) fulfilment, prophecy
    (c) purpose, possibly, misinterpreted
    (d) reflection/reflexion, turbulent   (e) fascinating, perturbing
    (f) argument, developed, logically   (g) definite
    (h) certain, aggressive   (i) foregoing, passage
    (j) attempt, devine   (k) there, perceived

Chapter 13, page 104: Vague expression and bad syntax (suggested alternatives)
    (a) From our position as observers, their lack of awareness of the outcome is tragic.
    (b) By writing *Sansibar*, Andersch affirms this commitment to humanity.
    (c) Zweig is a compassionate author, who sees people's strengths and weaknesses.
    (d) Here is another obvious aspect of Brecht's political stand.
    (e) The background is another aspect of the work, which impresses by its accuracy.
    (f) The complex style of Brecht's plays can make them seem difficult.
    (g) The two plays are very similar in theme and presentation.
    (h) Thomas Mann's use of language reflects his ironic view of life.
    (i) There is a unity about Goethe's work.
    (j) As he is a soldier returning after the war, it is perhaps inevitable that he thinks of the girl in the next room.
    (k) Keller clearly felt the need to expose this underlying characteristic, as a consequence of his observation of society.
    (l) This reveals her sarcastic reaction to the middle-classes.
    (m) Anna Seghers is a committed communist writer.

Chapter 13, page 105: Popular and slang expression (suggested alternatives)

(a) Gustav von Aschenbach prospers from his artistic endeavours.

(b) One has the impression that Dürrenmatt places Bärlach in a position from which he cannot win.

(c) 'Der Mann mit den Messern' exposes the reality of life in Germany at the end of the war.

(d) 'Die Dame am Steuer' drives like a woman possessed.

(e) Taugenichts is living in a perpetual state of euphoria.

(f) Eventually, it all becomes too irritating for Joseph K.

(g) Karl-Heinz needs to be pushed into action.

(h) The hero always wants to be on the move.

(i) The meeting is something of a nightmare.

(j) Whether she does it, is in the balance.

(k) Egmont has been greatly pressurised by Alba.

(l) Grete's situation is an unhappy one.

(m) Predictably, Jochen's behaviour becomes neurotic.

(n) Ludwig's behaviour reaches its lowest point.

(o) The story may bring tears to the reader's eyes.

Chapter 13, page 105: Cliché and nothing-statements (suggested alternatives)

(a) Christa Wolf has an ability for conveying the essence of the situation.

(b) The inspector arrives with the minimum of delay.

(c) Reinhardt Mey has a beautiful voice.

(d) Katya is a reliable, compassionate and maternal woman.

(e) Udo is by far the most sensitive of all the group.

(f) Greck finds himself unsuited to army life.

(g) Karl is utterly sadistic.

(h) Their ultimate happiness is never really threatened, as their love is strong enough to overcome their many difficulties.

(i) The Jewess is spared, because she sings so beautifully.

(j) The atmoshpere is so tense, that we are in the same state as the characters.

(k) Benno would be well advised to think before acting.

(l) Hölderlin's poetry shows his feeling for and his control over the language he uses.

(m) Thomas Mann's prose is rich in imagery, perhaps to reflect the symbolical nature of much of our behaviour.

Chapter 13, page 105: Involved writing (suggested fair-copies)

(a) Thomas Mann's style in *Der Tod in Venedig* may rightly be described as having a dense quality. This he often achieves through indulging his love of symbol, classical allusion, extended allegory and erudition. He uses these as a means of conveying not only the artist's predicament, but, with it, the complex inter-relationship of the intellectual, spiritual and physical worlds. In so doing, Mann allows the non-artist, normally unaware of the conflicting forces to which the artistic temperament is prey, to glean some notion of this inter-relationship.

(b) To me, Goethe's poetry is important, not simply for its lyricism, innovation, energy and imagery, but also for its clear presentation of the end of the old and the beginning of the Modern Age. This New Age is perceived by a man of exceptional feeling and intellect, with a natural radicalism. In much of his poetry, he makes conscious use of his revolutionary fervour and of his empathy for mankind, a mixture which is strongly conveyed by his outburst in *Prometheus*.

(c) Whether Anna Seghers may be regarded as a truly universal writer, depends on the reader's assessment of the political perspective in her work. We have to ask ourselves whether her frequently expressed admiration for Eastern European socialism and her criticism of the decadent right are presented with sufficient moderation for us to be able to keep in mind her more universal qualities. These are, of course, the breadth of her view of human nature and her ability to present the essence of a situation. The question is, does she allow the Western reader to feel that she is much more than an East German writer, writing for an East German public?

(d) If we are to ask ourselves what is the basis of Christa Wolf's own, particular art, then we are setting ourselves a task requiring precise and sensitive analysis. This is because she is a writer whose method is often exceptionally subtle. Her delineation of apparently life-like situations allows her readers to suspend their disbelief and her method turns on what we might call the concealment of art. To this end, she relies principally on devices such as understatement and the use of gentle humour.

Chapter 13, page 106: Repetition (suggested alternatives)
   (a) Stefan Zweig's strength lies in psychological character description. He studies the behaviour of the mind and gives each of his creations a full and rich personality.
   (b) Probably, we have here the likely motive.
   (c) This statement shows her skill as an observer.
   (d) Assuming this to be the case, we presume it is a reflection of his background.
   (e) This is, in fact, the first time he occasions actual bodily harm.
   (f) She has an eye for detail, is influenced by her memories of childhood and uses these to provide a series of cameos.
   (g) This perception allows for sensitive description, since the author's purpose in the work is to describe states of mind.
   (h) It is at this point that we understand the level to which she has sunk.
   (i) He considers alternatives, such as regarding himself as the devil's representative.
   (j) She is a perceptive author, who is aware of the essence of the human predicament.

Chapter 13, page 107: Over-verbalization (suggested alternatives)
  (a) Because her prose is so artfully simple, the author manages to obtain the reader's complete emotional involvement.
  (b) The reader, the vicarious observer, represents humanity watching life as it passes fleetingly by.
  (c) We find such a character wholly objectionable, as he reaches his lowest point and responds so negatively.
  (d) How can the reader find the central point of the work, when the author is so fond of obscuring his purpose?
  (e) The author-reader relationship is based on mutual dependence.
  (f) The way the author borrows from a variety of sources, is seen clearly in her description of atmosphere and environment.
  (g) The novel has been constructed, so that its stages correspond exactly to the stops and starts in the progress of the main character.
  (h) Despite the character's far-sightedness, his delight in misfortune is no basis for action.

Chapter 13, page 107: Grammatical inaccuracy
  (a) who have   (b) between Greta and him   (c) spring
  (d) fewer   (e) becomes clearer   (f) hanged   (g) for whom
  (h) no one has   (i) there are
  (j) While he was writing all his books, . . .

Questions on authors and general questions

ANDERSCH

1 How far does a knowledge of Andersch's own life help us in our understanding of *Sansibar oder der letzte Grund*?

2 Comment fully on the success or otherwise of Andersch's use of an episodic technique in *Sansibar oder der letzte Grund*.

3 Discuss the view that *der lesende Klosterschüler* may be regarded as the main character in *Sansibar oder der letzte Grund*.

4 Compare and contrast the characters and personalities of Gregor and Knudsen in *Sansibar oder der letzte Grund*.

5 What do you really understand to be 'the final reason' in *Sansibar oder der letzte Grund*?

6 Analyse the importance of the form and style of *Sansibar oder der letzte Grund*.

7 What does *Die Kirschen der Freiheit* tell us of Andersch's reasons for writing *Sansibar oder der letzte Grund*?

8 To what extent may *Die Kirschen der Freiheit* be regarded as a personal and factual Bildungsroman?

9 'Er liest alles, was er will. Weil er alles liest, was er will, sollte er eingesperrt werden. Und deswegen muß er jetzt wohin, wo er lesen kann, soviel er will.' Discuss with reference to *Sansibar oder der letzte Grund*.

BORCHERT

1 Given the fact that *Draußen vor der Tür* was written in anger, bewilderment and disillusionment, why should it still have such a strong hold on us today?

2 From your reading of *Draußen vor der Tür*, what is Borchert's view of the human condition in immediate post-war Germany?

3 What are the qualities in *Draußen vor der Tür*, which might make us regret Borchert's dying so shortly after having written it?

4 'Du siehst alles durch deine Gasmaskenbrille. Du siehst alles verbogen, Beckmann.' From your knowledge of *Draußen vor der Tür*, discuss the significance of this quotation both for the play and its author.

BÖLL

1 How far do you agree that *Und sagte kein einziges Wort* is more than just a piece of 'Trümmerliteratur'?

2 To what extent does Böll's feeling for the ordinary soldier express itself in *Wo warst du, Adam*?

3 Do you agree with the assessment of *Das Brot der frühen Jahre* as a 'love-story without true love'?

4 Analyse what Böll has to say about the relationship between society and the individual in *Das Brot der frühen Jahre*.

5 What do we learn about adolescents and their parents in *Im Tal der donnernden Hufe*?

6 How far does Böll succeed in stating and resolving the problems of the modern state in *Die verlorene Ehre der Katharina Blum*?

7 From your reading of *Die verlorene Ehre der Katharina Blum*, what do you discern to be Böll's view of the role of the press in modern society?

8 'Die Geschichte zweier Menschen, die an den Vorurteilen und Maßstäben unserer Gesellschaft scheitern.' Discuss the accuracy of this description of *Ansichten eines Clowns*.

9 'Eines der wichtigsten Bücher unserer deutschen Gegenwart.' Do you concur or not with this judgement of *Billard um halb zehn*? Provide a reasoned argument for the position you hold.

10 'Trotz der Vielfalt seines literarischen Werks, haben seine Romane und Erzählungen eines gemeinsam: Das Eintreten für die Zurückgekommenen, die Außenseiter und die ewig Machtlosen in unserer Gesellschaft.' Discuss with reference to any one or more of Böll's major works.

BRECHT

1 Asses Brecht's attitude to his major women characters in either *Mutter Courage, Der gute Mensch von Sezuan* or *Der kaukasische Kreidekreis*.

2 Analyse the effect of Brecht's dramatic technique in *Leben des Galilei*.

3 Assess the consistency with which Brecht adheres to the *Verfremdungseffekt* in any of his major plays.

4 'Dramatist, novelist, poet, musician – the man has almost too much talent.' Discuss this judgement on Brecht.

5 From your reading of *Die Kalendergeschichten*, in what ways may Brecht be regarded as a didactic writer?

6 Discuss the effect of Brecht's long period of exile on his work.

7 'Wirklich, ich lebe in finsteren Zeiten! Das arglose Wort ist töricht.' What light does this comment throw on any of Brecht's major works?

8 'Brecht should be seen and not read!' Discuss with reference to any one or two of the dramatist's major works.

DROSTE-HÜLSHOFF

1 What are the strengths of Droste-Hülshoff's poetry, that she should achieve such eminence, when the published German-speaking poets were predominantly male?

2 What are the essentially feminine qualities of Droste-Hülshoff's poetry?

3 To what extent do you agree with the dismissive comment that Droste-Hülshoff should have stayed writing poetry and left *Die Judenbuche* unwritten?

4 How fair would it be to call *Die Judenbuche* a realistic work?

5 How far do you support the judgement that Friedrich Mergel in *Die Judenbuche* is 'guilty, but with diminished responsibility'?

6 Analyse, with suitable quotations, the main points of Droste-Hülshoff's poetic style.

7 'So steht mein Entschluß fester als jemals, nie auf Effekt zu arbeiten, keiner beliebten Manier, keinem andern als der ewig wahren Natur durch die Windung des Menschenherzens zu folgen und unserer blasierten Zeit den Rücken zuzuwenden.' How valid is this comment by Droste-Hülshoff on her own poetic work?

DÜRRENMATT

1 What did Dürrenmatt mean, when he referred to *Der Besuch der alten Dame* as 'eine Komödie der Hochkonjunktur'?

2 How valid is the judgement, that 'in Dürrenmatt's plays, we see a succession of cardboard characters, taking up postures'?

3 What impression do we gain of the forces of good and evil from Dürrenmatt's detective novels?

4 List and comment on the major points of Dürrenmatt's style in his novels.

5 'An improbable plot with implausible characters.' To what extent would you concur with this rejection of *Der Richter und sein Henker*?

6 'Dürrenmatt should have left detective novels to the detective writers!' Discuss.

EICHENDORFF

1 '*Wanderlust*, all is *Wanderlust!*' Discuss this comment in relation to *Aus dem Leben eines Taugenichts.*

2 Analyse the significance of the 'ICH' narrative in *Aus dem Leben eines Taugenichts.*

3 Discuss the roles of Aurelie, Rosette, Flora, and Leonardo in relation to Taugenichts.

4 Discuss the view that *Taugenichts* is a deceptively simple work.

5 Assess the character and role of Taugenichts within *Aus dem Leben eines Taugenichts.*

6 'Es ist etwas Adeliges in dem Helden.' Comment on Eichendorff's own words on Taugenichts.

FONTANE

1 Assess how the religious and social background in *Grete Minde* affects her decisions and fosters her demise.

2 Which methods does Fontane use to maintain our sympathy for Grete?

3 How and why does Fontane convey to the reader the impression that Grete Minde's fate is inevitable?

4 Analyse the essentials of the relationships shared by Grete, Gerdt and Trud in *Grete Minde.*

5 'Ich mag kein Unrecht sehen und auch keines leiden.' How far does this statement by Grete explain her character and her fortunes?

FRISCH

1 What is modern about Frisch's treatment of the Don Juan legend in *Don Juan oder die Liebe zur Geometrie?*

2 Analyse the function and effectiveness of Frisch's use of historical figures in *Die chinesische Mauer.*

3 Analyse the significance of the playing of false roles in any of Frisch's major works.

4 Comment on Frisch's choice of the name 'Biedermann' for one of the principals in *Biedermann und die Brandstifter.*

5 Comment on Frisch's dramatic technique and its effect on our appreciation of *Biedermann und die Brandstifter.*

6 'Frisch's work is more Swiss than German.' What do you think is meant by this comment?

7 'Du zuckst die Achsel. Das ist alles! Die Achsel zucken und eine nächste Zigarette anzünden, während sie einen Stummen foltern und zum Schreien bringen.' How accurate is Mee Lan's assessment of Der Heutige's behaviour and function in *Die chinesische Mauer*?

GOETHE

1 'Es erbt der Eltern Segen, nicht ihr Fluch.'
'Es fürchte die Götter das Menschengeschlecht.'
Comment on these two statements as expressions of Goethe's Weltanschauung.

2 Illustrate the significance of Nature in Goethe's lyric poetry up to 1775.

3 'Goethe cannot really have believed in so crazily anti-social an ideal as that of *Götz*; it has no relation to actual life either in his own day or in ours.' Discuss.

4 Discuss the view that Egmont embodies the German obsession with the death-wish.

5 How far do you find Klärchen to be a satisfactory character in *Egmont*?

6 What justification is there in the claim that Egmont is responsible for his own downfall?

7 Comment on the significance of the Gefängnis scene in *Egmont*. How far may the success of the play be said to turn on it?

8 It has often been said that the Sturm und Drang is characterised by its authors' zeal to put things to right, single-handed. How far can you apply this view to any one or more of Goethe's plays?

9 'In the thoughts and feelings expressed by *Egmont, Iphegenie auf Tauris, Torquato Tasso*, there is something factitious; something devised and determined by the thinker, not given by the necessity of nature herself.' Consider this assessment in relation to any one or more of the plays.

10 What for you is the main theme of Goethe's *Faust I*? Estimate its significance in terms of human experience.

11 Analyse the conflict between Faust and Mephistopheles in *Faust I*.

GRASS

1 From your reading of any major work by Grass, explain why he may be regarded as an essentially political writer.

2 Assess the effect of Grass's religious upbringing on any one of his major works.

3 Why does Grass regard *Katz und Maus* as a Novelle rather than a Roman?

4 Analyse in detail the main features of Grass's narrative technique, as exemplified in any one of his major works.

5 Discuss the use made by Grass of 'sein geliebtes Danziger Platt' in his work.

6 'The main impression one gains from the work of Günter Grass is his obsession with Danzig!' Discuss, with close reference to the text(s) you have studied.

7 What is the basic conflict that Grass attempts to resolve in his work?

8 Assess the literary merit of *Die Blechtrommel*.

9 In what ways is Günter Grass a committed author?

10 Compare *Örtlich Betäubt* with *Katz und Maus*.

GRILLPARZER

1 From what does tragedy spring in Grillparzer's tragedies?

2 Compare and contrast *Die Ahnfrau* and *Sappho*.

3 '*Das goldene Vlieβ* may fairly be claimed as the finest of all dramatic versions of the Greek saga.' Do you agree?

4 How far do you concur with the view that *Das goldene Vlieβ* is essentially a modern tragedy?

5 'Not the least remarkable feature of Grillparzer's genius is the rich diversity of his plays.' Comment on the significance of this assessment for at least two of Grillparzer's works.

6 Grillparzer's overriding concern in life was with 'des Innern stillen Frieden'. How is this concern exemplified in *Der Traum ein Leben*?

7 'Erst Grillparzer hat durch sein Hinzutreten aus dem verschiedenfarbigen Zweiklang Goethe und Schiller den harmonischen und vollkommenen Dreiklang der klassischen Dichtung deutscher Sprache gemacht . . .' Discuss with reference to any one or more of Grillparzer's major dramas.

HAUPTMANN

1 Why is *Bahnwärter Thiel* often regarded as something of a disturbing work?

2 Comment on the character and role of Thiel in this Novelle.

3 Compare and contrast *Bahnwärter Thiel* and *Fasching* from the point of view of style and treatment of themes.

4 Trace the influence of Ibsen, Tolstoy and Zola on any of Hauptmann's early works.

5 Analyse the reasons why *Vor Sonnenaufgang* should have provoked such controversy when it first appeared.

6 Analyse those elements of any early work by Hauptmann, which were particularly naturalistic.

7 From your reading of any or of all of *Vor Sonnenaufgang, das Friedensfest* and *Einsame Menschen*, what do you learn of Hauptmann's attitude to family relationships at this time?

8 '*Die Weber* was an achievement, both in the literary and the political sense.' Discuss.

9 Examine the significance of Mutter Wolff in *Der Biberpelz*.

10 How do you equate *Hanneles Himmelfahrt* with Hauptmann's earlier work?

11 Account for the considerable popularity which *Die versunkene Glocke* achieved in Germany.

HEBBEL

1 Analyse the main source of tragedy in Hebbel's drama.

2 Assess the relationship of ethical guilt and tragic guilt in any one or more plays by Hebbel.

3 How has Hebbel given new life to the biblical tale of Judith and Holofernes?

4 Discuss the view that 'the will, nothing but the unredeemed and uncompromising will, was Hebbel's innermost concern' with reference to any one or more of his plays.

5 Comment on the points of similarity and variance in the way Hebbel and Shakespeare construct the characters of their heroes.

HEINE

1 Discuss the use made by Heine of the Romantic *Sehnsucht* motif.

2 What is there in Heine's poetry that makes him such a controversial author?

3 Heine has often been described as a master of poetic device. Using appropriate quotation, show how far you agree or disagree with this view.

4 Account for Heine's popularity with the British reading-public.

5 'Trotz meiner exterminatorischen Feldzüge gegen die Romantik blieb ich doch selbst immer ein Romantiker . . . ' Assess the validity of Heinrich Heine's own judgement on himself.

HOFMANNSTHAL

1 What do you understand by the term 'Prä-existenz,' as applied to Hofmannsthal's early work?

2 Is the description of Hofmannsthal's *Der Turm* as 'his last will and testament' a fair one? Illustrate your answer with appropriate quotations.

3 How does Hofmannsthal use *Der Schwierige* to re-present the problem with which he first exercised himself in the *Chandos Brief*?

4 What is especially Viennese about Hofmannsthal's method, style and preoccupations in his work?

5 'The *Kleine Dramen* are unplayable!' Discuss.

KAFKA

1 List and analyse the main themes unifying Kafka's short stories.

2 'Kafka's work deals with a crisis of awareness – his own and ours.' Discuss.

3 What are the hallmarks of Kafka's style?

4 Discuss in some detail the roles of the supporting characters in *Der Prozeß* or *Das Schloß*.

5 'Kafka owes more than a small debt to Lewis Caroll and his *Alice in Wonderland*.' Comment on this assessment of Franz Kafka.

6 'This is a rather Kafka-esque situation' is a cliché of our time. Assess the significance of this cliché in relation to any major work of Kafka's that you have read.

7 'Für Kafka steht der Mensch in der paradoxen, absurden Situation zwischen Leben und Tod . . . ' How far do you agree with this comment on Kafka's work?

KAISER

1 How just or unjust is it to describe Kaiser's drama as 'dated Expressionism'?

2 How does Kaiser maintain the dramatic tension in *Die Bürger von Calais*?

3 Examine *Die Bürger von Calais* as a study in conflict.

4 Analyse the dramatic techniques employed by Kaiser in *Die Bürger von Calais*.

5 Discuss the view that, in our nuclear age, the trilogy *Gas* has a re-discovered meaning.

6 In what ways may Eustache de Saint Pierre be said to incorporate the ideal of 'der neue Mensch' in *Die Bürger von Calais*?

7 'Mit keinem Geld aus allen Bankkassen der Welt kann man sich irgendwas von Wert kaufen.' Analyse the importance of this quotation for our understanding of *Von morgens bis mitternachts*.

KELLER

1 Discuss the view that 'all Keller's stories suggest that he was a humane and tolerant man with a sense of humour.'

2 What evidence is there in any of Keller's work that you have read of his early training as an artist?

3 Comment on Keller's use of irony in his work.

4 How true is it to say that Keller's attitude towards the Bürgertum is at best ambiguous?

5 'Ich bin nicht ganz so, wie ich scheine!' Assess the underlying reasons for Wenzel's mistaken identity in *Kleider machen Leute*.

6 '*Kleider machen Leute* is a masterpiece of precision.' Discuss.

KLEIST

1 What features in any play(s) you have read by Kleist confirm the often expressed opinion that he is the most powerful of German playwrights?

2 How far do you agree with the view that '*Der zerbrochene Krug* is neither comic nor drama'?

3 In what ways may Kleist be said to have been resolving his own predicament in *Prinz Friedrich von Homburg*?

4 Give a critical appraisal of Kleist as a story-teller.

5 How may the main characters in Kleist's stories be regarded as victims, in a state of perplexity?

SIEGFRIED LENZ

1 Analyse the relationship between Carla and Bert in *Brot und Spiele*.

2 Comment on the fundamentals of the relationship between the narrator and the hero in *Brot und Spiele*.

3 Which gifts do you think Lenz has brought to the specifically German genre of the *Hörspiel*?

4 'Wir passen nicht zueinander. Das habe ich gelernt, als ich bei euch war.' Examine the learning process to which Lena refers in *Der Mann im Strom*.

5 From your reading of Siegfried Lenz, in what ways may he be said to be specifically relevant to our modern age?

LESSING

1 How far are you in agreement with the statement, that 'it is clear from *Nathan* that Lessing was interested in religion primarily as a means of propagating standards of humane conduct among men'?

2 What justification is there for the view that Emilia may not be altogether the main character in *Emilia Galotti*?

3 Assess Lessing's portrayal of the Prince in *Emilia Galotti*.

4 To what extent may *Emilia Galotti* be regarded as a confrontation between the polarised forces of good and evil?

5 'Verführung ist die wahre Gewalt.' Discuss the significance of this quotation for our understanding of *Emilia Galotti*.

6 From your reading of Lessing, is it possible to view him as a characteristic representative of Enlightenment?

THOMAS MANN

1 Analyse the structure of either *Buddenbrooks* or *Der Zauberberg*.

2 For what reasons did Thomas Mann employ such a humorous style in *Felix Krull?*

3 'This comedy on *unauthentic living* is a parody of civilization itself.' Comment on this view of *Felix Krull*.

4 'Are Thomas Mann's artists outsiders because they are artists, or artists because they are outsiders'? Discuss with reference to any one or two of Thomas Mann's major works.

5 From your reading of Thomas Mann's work, why do you think he should have become known as 'the ironic German'?

6 To what extent do Tonio Kröger and Gustav von Aschenbach represent different stages in the same process?

7 'Das Bürgertum erschien ihm als Träger einer langen, beglückenden Tradition geistiger Werte . . .' Discuss with reference to any of Thomas Mann's major works.

MÖRIKE

1 What is the basic function of nature in Mörike's poetry?

2 How far may Mörike's life and his poetry be explained by his relationship with Maria Meyer?

3 Discuss with illustrations the characteristic features of Mörike's poetry.

4 'Mörike paints the reality of our internal world'. Discuss.

5 Explain, giving appropriate examples from the texts, why so much of Mörike's poetry should have been successfully set to music .

6 How far do you agree with the statement that 'Mörike's strength as a poet is his ability to create moods and communicate feelings'?

NOVALIS

1 'In der Geschichte des deutschen Romans nimmt *Heinrich von Ofterdingen* eine einzigartige Stellung ein.' Analyse the novel in the light of this comment.

2 In what sense may *Heinrich von Ofterdingen* be regarded as representative of early Romanticism?

3 Trace the effect of Sophie von Kühn on the *Hymnen an die Nacht.*

4 Analyse the relationship between religion and grief in *Hymnen an die Nacht.*

5 How far may *Heinrich von Ofterdingen* be regarded as allegorical and in relation to what?

6 List and illustrate the poetic devices used by Novalis.

REMARQUE

1 Analyse those qualities in *Im Westen nichts Neues*, which give it its universal implications.

2 How much attention does Remarque pay to character in *Im Westen nichts Neues*?

3 Compare and contrast *Im Westen nichts Neues* with any novel of the Second World War with which you are familiar.

4 What relevance does *Im Westen nichts Neues* have for a world living under the threat of nuclear war?

5 'Die erste Granate, die einschlug, traf in unser Herz . . . ' Precisely what significance does this statement by Paul Bäumer have for our understanding of *Im Westen nichts Neues?*

6 In what ways may *Im Westen nichts Neues* be said to stand out as the finest literary achievement of the period of the First World War?

SCHILLER

1 In what respects may any one or more plays by Schiller be said to be an exposition of the relationship between moral and tragic guilt?

2 How far do you consider Wallenstein to be a noble hero with a consequently tragic demise?

3 How does Schiller give Wilhelm moral credibility in *Wilhelm Tell?*

4 '*Die Räuber* intoxicates us with words, so that we do not see its weaknesses as a play.' Discuss the fairness of this comment.

5 Analyse Schiller's treatment of the theme of freedom in *Maria Stuart*.

6 How true is it to say that Maria has grown in moral stature by the end of *Maria Stuart*?

7 Discuss Schiller's use of history in *Maria Stuart*.

8 'Sterben ist nichts – doch *leben* und nicht *sehen*, das ist ein Unglück' Comment on any of Schiller's dramas in the light of this quotation from *Wilhelm Tell*.

9 Comment on the view that Schiller's lyric poetry is 'all *Sturm und Drang* and no *Geist*'.

SEGHERS

1 Identify and explain the underlying theme in the *Friedensgeschichten*.

2 Discuss the use Anna Seghers makes of the theme of the outsider/in-comer in her work.

3 Seghers' novels have been described as 'combative'. Comment on this aggressive quality in her work.

4 Using your study of her work as a basis, try to explain why an East German writer should have become so well-loved in the West.

5 What are the essential qualities of Seghers style? Illustrate your answer with close textual reference.

6 How far do you agree with the judgement that Anna Seghers' earlier, anti-Nazi writings are vastly superior to her later socialist novels?

SCHNITZLER

1 Discuss the view that *Reigen* is little more than 'an essay in voyeurism'.

2 For what reasons is *Reigen* enjoying a new vogue in our decade? Illustrate your answer with close reference to the text.

3 What do we learn from *Professor Bernhardi* of the political situation in Austria around 1900?

4 Examine the significance of Bernhardi's jewishness in *Professor Bernhardi*.

5 What are the main facets of Schnitzler's dramatic technique. Illustrate your answer with appropriate quotations.

6 Compare and contrast *Liebelei* and *Reigen*.

7 In what ways may Schnitzler be said to be 'the high-priest of naturalist drama in an age of decadence'?

8 Show what is essentially *fin de siècle* in Schnitzler's drama.

9 Discuss the view that 'Schnitzler is much more than a purveyor of soft porn. We should not ignore his knowledge and his skilful presentation of the advances in psychological research and analysis'.

STIFTER

1 What do we learn of Stifter's attitude to nature from *Bunte Steine?*

2 Discuss any of Stifter's works in relation to the term, 'poetic realism'.

3 From your reading of *Bergkristall*, what do you learn of contemporary rural life?

4 'Wir wollen das sanfte Gesetz zu erblicken versuchen, wodurch das menschliche Geschlecht geleitet wird.' From your reading of Stifter, what was 'das sanfte Gesetz' which preoccupied him?

STORM

1 What features of any major work by Storm may be regarded as poetic realism?

2 Assess the significance of Storm's love of his homeland for an understanding of his work.

3 How far do you concur with the view that to understand Storm's prose works, we should read his poetry?

4 Storm referred to the Novelle as 'die strengste und geschlossenste Form der Prosadichtung, die Schwester des Dramas'. Assess the relevance of this statement to any of the Novellen which you may have read.

5 How far are you in agreement with the description of *Immensee* as a 'lyrical Novelle'?

6 Analyse Storm's presentation of the institution of marriage in *Immensee*.

7 'Storm verharrt meist im Unentschiedenen.' Are you in agreement with this assessment?

WEDEKIND

1 What are the main features of Wedekind's short stories and *Novellen*?

2 Why has *Frühlings Erwachen* enjoyed a resurgence of popularity?

3 Assess the effectiveness of the structure of *Frühlings Erwachen*.

4 Analyse the conflict between the worlds of the adolescent and the adult in *Frühlings Erwachen*.

5 Of what significance is Wedekind's Austrian background for an understanding of his work?

6 'Wedekind should never have had anything to do with Freud!' Is this a fair judgement on *Erdgeist* and/or *Die Büchse der Pandora*?

7 Why should Wedekind's *Lulu* retain such a fascination for the modern theatre-goer and reader?

8 'Du weißt, daß ich keinem Manne gehören kann; ich bin von meinem Verhängnis nicht dazu bestimmt.' Analyse *Erdgeist* and/or *Die Büchse der Pandora* in the light of this comment by *Die Geschwitz*.

ZUCKMAYER

1 What do we learn of the conflict between the state and the individual in *Der Hauptmann von Köpenick*?

2 From your reading of *Der Hauptmann von Köpenick*, give an assessment of Zuckmayer's stage craft.

3 Given the satirical implications of *Der Hauptmann von Köpenick*, what is the significance of its gently humorous and affectionate conclusion?

4 'Na, das weiß doch ein Kind, daß man bei uns mit dem Militär alles machen kann.' Discuss the implications of Voigt's words for our understanding of *Der Hauptmann von Köpenick*.

5 *Des Teufels General* met instant success when it appeared in 1946. Why should this have been so?

6 Analyse the points of communality between *Des Teufels General* and *Der Hauptmann von Köpenick*.

7 What are the implications of Harras' opportunism for our understanding of *Des Teufels General*?

8 'Harras' greatest strength – his individualism – is also his greatest weakness.' In your judgement, how far is this a valid assessment?

9 Why should Zuckmayer and Brecht be regarded as the pinnacles of the twin poles of twentieth century German drama?

ZWEIG

1 For what reasons should Zweig now be regarded as one of the great writers in German in this twentieth century?

2 'Like Dickens, Zweig has a penchant for eccentric characters, but the use he makes of them is very different.' Discuss with reference to any of Zweig's *Novellen*.

3 'Diese besondere Liebe und Neugier für gefährdete Menschen hat mich übrigens mein ganzes Leben lang begleitet.' What light does this comment by Stefan Zweig shed on your understanding of any of his main characters?

4 Analyse the character and significance of Buchmendel.

5 From your reading of Zweig's Novellen, what do you deduce to be his main preoccupations?

6 Zweig has often been called a psychological writer. What do you understand by this? Illustrate your answer with copious textual reference.

GENERAL POETRY QUESTIONS

1 Discuss the attitude of any Romantic poet to the world of finite experience.

2 Analyse the characteristics of Eichendorff's/Uhland's/Lenau's poetic style.

3 Discuss the view that Eichendorff's poetry is, like his novel, deceptively simple.

4 In what ways may Hölderlin be said to be a complex poet?

5 What is there about Brentano that makes his lyric poetry of more than historical importance?

6 Write an introduction to Rilke's lyric poetry.

7 In what ways may Stefan George be regarded as a reformist poet?

8 Comment on the theme of isolation in the work of Heym/Trakl and/or Benn.

9 Discuss the view that Brecht's success as a dramatist obscures the genius of his poetry.

10 Comment on the dignified quality of Hans Carossa's poetry.

GENERAL LITERATURE AND BACKGROUND QUESTIONS

1 Review any work you have read, which presents an optimistic or satisfied view of the society it depicts.

2 Outline the political, religious and social background to German Naturalism.

3 Compare any two German works you have read, the major theme of which is a strong criticism of society.

4 Produce a critical review of a modern German novel of your choice, drawing your readership's attention to the way in which contemporary society is presented.

5 Discuss, with close reference to at least one text you have studied, the conflict between the aspirations of the individual and the demands of society.

6 Referring specifically to one of your set texts, consider how literature can extend your historical awareness.

7 Comment on the resolution of the theme of historical guilt, as seen in the work of any post-war German writer.

8 What does German Expressionism tell us about contemporary German society?

9 Analyse any emerging author's view of our present society.

10 What lessons do you find to be intrinsic in any work you have read, relating to either the First or the Second World War?

11 For what reasons have there been so few eminent women writers in the German language? To what extent is the situation now changing?

12 Compare the attitudes to society reflected in the work of one East and one West German writer.